Claudia Saglimbeni

essays by

Laura Andreini
Silvia Malcovati
Benedikt Goebel
Bernd Albers

ON THE ROAD city
Berlin

ON THE ROAD
editor of collection
Laura Andreini

editorial project
Forma Edizioni srl, Firenze, Italia
redazione@formaedizioni.it
www.formaedizioni.it

editorial direction
Laura Andreini

authors
Claudia Saglimbeni

editorial staff
Maria Giulia Caliri
Livia D'Aliasi
Raffaele Moretti
Elena Varani

graphic design
Isabella Peruzzi

translations
Katy Hannan
Karen Tomatis

photolithography
Forma Edizioni

texts by
Laura Andreini
Silvia Malcovati
Benedikt Goebel
Bernd Albers

Claudia Saglimbeni, grew up in Italy and Brazil.
She took her degree in Architecture at Politecnico
University, Milan, followed by an Executive
Master's degree in European Museology from
IULM University, Milan. She has had a long
career as freelance Project Manager and Curator,
developing and coordinating publishing projects,
events, exhibitions, museum curation, and
communication projects in design, architecture,
art and culture, as well as for the food, fashion,
automotive and mobility sectors. She headed the
strategic consulting department as Senior Curator
at the Luca Molinari Studio, and is co-founder
of the travelling exhibition, *Migrant Garden*.
She writes for several Italian and international
magazines on architecture, design and fashion.
She teaches Project Planning courses at the
Politecnico universities of Milan and Turin.

unless otherwise specified:
photos
© Denis Esakov

First Edition: May 2022

ISBN 978-88-55210-56-0

Table of contents

Guidebook as a tool

On the Road is a collection of contemporary architecture guidebooks whose purpose is to tell about a place, whether a city or larger area, through its architectural works chosen to be visited and experienced directly.

The guidebook has a convenient special jacket that opens into a map marking the location of the architectural works and interesting sites to visit. On the back are miniature images and addresses of the architectural works described in detail within.

The book starts with short essays explaining the city or area's present day and history and outlining possible future scenarios with planned or imminent projects. Each work features a photograph of the whole, an architectural drawing (plan or section), a short description, and facts including architect, type, year of construction, address, website, and how to visit it.

The finest architecture of each city and suggested routes are represented by this collection of not-to-be-missed, "timeless" buildings that uniquely define their settings. General information and useful tips for travelers help them optimize their visits and quickly understand the essence of the place described.

Museums, theatres, restaurants, hotels and a list of top architectural firms working in the city let visitors turn a regular trip into an opportunity for study or work.

Note: The pinpoints outside the maps at the beginning of the itineraries are viewable on the rear of the book jacket.

Berlin

Laura Andreini*

The On the Road architectural guide series would not be complete without a book describing Berlin. Visitors to Berlin are rapidly aware of the experimental urban planning and architecture implemented in recent decades in a city that encapsulates 20th century European history in just a few square kilometres.

Berlin could easily be considered as a synecdoche, the rhetorical figure where one aspect represents a complete whole, such as Germany, or even Europe in general. Here, politics and architecture initially tried to cancel the powerful and painful traces left by history.

In Berlin, the architectural design process first destroyed, then rebuilt, then gradually made its peace with a burdensome past, integrating it within the urban fabric that was forcibly divided, disoriented during the process of reunification, and finally enthusiastic as it lives with the impressive results.

Like the other major cities featured in this book series, the urban lay-out was divided into five separate itineraries that can be visited on foot, by bicycle, or by subway. In addition, among the buildings included, readers will notice several iconic examples of Modern architecture that are instrumental landmarks for finding one's bearings: works by famous architects like Mies van der Rohe, Le Corbusier, Walter Gropius, Bruno Taut, to name just a few.

Those who have been lucky enough to visit Berlin several times over the past thirty years will have noticed its massive transformation: a divided city before the fall of the Berlin wall, the countless construction sites during the late nineties, and today, a metropolis that proclaims its unique identity, bolstered by the transformations it has undergone and welcomed.

Germany's capital is a city of great interest for those with a passion for contemporary architecture: strongly dynamic, contemporary, non conventional design whose rules were established as projects were developed in the city. A visit to Berlin provides architecture lovers with an opportunity for close-up contact with design called upon to resolve enormous problems based not only on the physical size of the projects, but also for the vast political and social issues involved. Visitors will be filled with enthusiasm on feeling the impact of the city's resourceful ideas.

* Laura Andreini is Architect and Associate Professor at DIDA, University of Florence. Co-founder of Studio Archea where she still works, she is also writer and deputy editor for *area* magazine.

Political / geographical facts

country
Germany

language
german

area code
+49 30

coordinates
52° 31' 27 N
13° 24' 37 E

area
891,8 km²

population
3,748,000

density
4,165.47 inhab./km²

time zone
UTC+1

city website
www.berlin.de

Administrative districts
1. Charlottenburg-Wilmersdorf
2. Friedrichshain-Kreuzberg
3. Lichtenberg
4. Marzahn-Hellersdorf
5. Mitte
6. Neukölln
7. Pankow
8. Reinickendorf
9. Spandau
10. Steglitz-Zehlendorf
11. Tempelhof-Schöneberg
12. Treptow-Köpenick

General information
useful addresses and numbers

INFORMATION OFFICES

www.visitberlin.de
tel +49 30 25002333

Berlin Tourist Info im Hauptbahnhof
Erdgeschoss/ Eingang Europaplatz,
10557 Berlin
+49 30 250025
Mon - Sun / 10 am - 6 pm

Berlin Tourist Info im Brandenburger Tor
Pariser Platz 1, 10117 Berlin
+49 30 250025
April - October / November - March
Mon - Sun / 10 am - 6 pm

Berlin Tourist Info im Europa-Center
Tauentzienstraße 9, 10789 Berlin
+49 30 250025
Mon - Sat / 10 am - 8 pm

**Berlin Tourist Info im Park Inn
am Alexanderplatz**
Alexanderplatz 7, 10178 Berlin
+49 30 250025
Mon - Sun / 10 am - 6 pm

Berlin Tourist Info im Flughafen Tegel
Saatwinkler Damm, 13405 Berlin
+49 30 25002333
Mon - Sun / 10 am - 6 pm

EMERGENCY SERVICES

Police 110
**Accident & Emergency,
Emergency Doctor
and Fire Department** 112

URBAN TRANSPORT*

**Subway, urban railway line, bus
and tram services**
The Berlin transport system is divided into three
zones in concentric circles: Zone A covers the area
as far as the S-Bahn ring and includes the city
centre. Zone B covers the area out to the city limits,
and Zone C covers the outer suburbs of Berlin.
Tickets can be bought from numerous BVG or
S-Bahn network vendors in Berlin or directly from
automatic distributors at stations.

Taxi
Radio Cab Berlin 26 10 26: +49 30 261026
Radio Cab Berlin: +49 30 3416908
Taxi Berlin: +49 30 202020

Car sharing
ShareNow, DriveNow, SIXT Share, Car2go, Miles

Bike rental
Donkey Republic, Rent a Bike 44, Berlin on Bike

EMBASSY OF THE UNITED STATES OF AMERICA
Pariser Platz 2, 10117 Berlin
Tel +49 30 83050

BRITISH EMBASSY
Wilhelmstraße 70/71, 10117 Berlin
Tel +49 30 204570

ITALIAN EMBASSY
Hiroshimastraße 1, 10785 Berlin
Tel +49 30 254400

EMBASSY OF THE PEOPLE'S REPUBLIC OF CHINA
Märkisches Ufer 54, 10179 Berlin
Tel +49 30 275880

FRENCH EMBASSY
Pariser Platz 5, 10117 Berlin
Tel +49 30 590039000

HOW TO PHONE

From a local landline: enter the phone number only,
including the city area code (030)

From a foreign landline: enter the international
code (+49), city area code (30) and the phone
number

* Ticket categories:
Zone AB / One way trip: 2,80 €; reduced price; 1,70 €
Short distances: 1,70 €; reduced price: 1,30 €
Zone ABC / One way trip: 3,40 €; reduced price: 2,50 €

Daily ticket: 7,00 €; reduced price: 4,70 €
Weekly ticket: 30,00 €
4 trip ticket: 9,00 €
Group ticket (max 5 people): 19,90 €

Useful tips

1. Berlin offers a vast selection of **accommodation** ranging from cheap hostels to trendy boutique hotels. Apart from the centre, Mitte, without a doubt the most popular area is Kreuzberg, and on the other side of the River Spree, Friedrichshain. Along Warschauer Straße, there are large numbers of hotels and hostels to suit every budget. In addition, the Prenzlauer Berg quarter is very dynamic, with a vibrant night life and trendy stores and clubs, above all ideal for the younger generation.

2. Rule number one: **go by bike**. It is not really worth taking a taxi in Berlin since there are countless, much cheaper forms of transport. It is very easy to rent a bicycle, and they can often be rented from the hotel where you stay. Public transport connects every corner of the city and runs 24 hours a day during the weekends. Berlin is a very safe city and visitors will find the stations full of people at any time, day or night. If you feel the need to take a taxi without spending too much, you can take the "limited budget" option: tell the driver how much money you want to spend and he will stop when you have finished your budget. We recommend that visitors take the time to stroll and wander around the different quarters. Stop and look at the **Stolpersteine**, or "stumbling stones", slightly raised, inscribed brass cobblestones, bearing the names of concentration camp victims. This monumental European project was launched by Gunter Demnig as a memorial to those who died in the camps.

3. It would be unthinkable to cross Berlin without a special visit to the East Side Gallery in Mühlenstraße, the section where the **Berlin Wall** overlooks the River Spree. This is an open-air museum, one and a half kilometres long, covered by more than a hundred art works by street artists and writers from all over the world to celebrate the new winds of freedom and reconciliation. Among the most famous are *The Mortal Kiss* by Dmitri Vrubel, depicting the kiss between Brežnev and Honecker, and *Test the best* by Birgit Kinder showing the Trabant, symbolic auto of the GDR.

4. Berlin has always been the capital of electronic **music** and the most avant-garde scene for independent culture. To capture the essence of this city, visitors need to spend at least one night in a Berlin club. Well worth a visit is the RAW Gelände/Tempel, the main alternative cultural scene in Berlin, open 24 hours a day. It was occupied in 1999, and features the Cassiopeia and Badehaus bands in alternating evenings of electronic, jazz, and punk music as well as metal and hip hop; Urban Spree is a club, gallery and bar with a program that changes in continuation. Do not miss the area around Rosenthaler Platz, a blend of street food stalls, discotheques, live clubs and movie theatres, especially the Shokoladen, Berlin musicians' favourite club for jazz, punk and indie rock. To hear some great electronic and techno music, the best address is the Berghain/Panorama Bar (more exclusive). Housed in a former abandoned train depot, it is notorious for the very tough selection at the entrance. The famous Tresor club occupies a former power plant; the Sisyphos: an ex-biscuit factory now converted into a double space club behind the river; and the Watergate, with full-height windows overlooking the water.

5. History is present everywhere in Berlin, but there are some less famous **museums** that are not featured among the buildings in this guide, but which are well worth a visit, like the more recent Checkpoint Charlie sites, the Hohenschönhausen prison, or the GDR museum. The Topography of Terror is located in the ex-Gestapo secret police headquarters next to the Gropius Bau, a short walk from Potsdamer Platz. It is a museum dedicated to photos, maps, and top secret documents that bear witness to the terror system applied by the Nazis during the darkest years of European history. 15 stations form an outdoor exhibition, and another exhibition can be visited from Spring to Autumn in another site in Niederkirchnerstraße, along the remains of the buried walls, which have now been uncovered.

6. Berlin's **parks and public spaces** come alive as soon as the warm weather arrives. Families and young people have picnics or an aperitif along the banks of the River Spree, where it is common to see ferry party boats with music playing full blast. On Sundays, certain parks hold urban markets: the largest and most popular are at the Mauerpark or the Tiergartenpark.

Berlin before 1710: Civic town and royal residence

Benedikt Goebel*

An important city, mentioned for the first time 2000 years after the foundation of Rome, with an historic old town a mere quarter of a square kilometre in size, in the centre of which only 12 buildings that pre-date 1710 remain standing? Is such a metropolis conceivable? Berlin is indeed such a city. Although it cannot be termed a metropolis in the true sense of the word, since it not only has a mother city (Brandenburg an der Havel), but even a grandmother city (Magdeburg). Brandenburg an der Havel and Magdeburg are, figuratively speaking, the Trojan prince Aeneas and the suckling she-wolf to Berlin. For cities that are so young that they demonstrably received their city charter from other cities do not require mythology to explain their foundation. Instead, they come into being because, for example, the local sovereign and bishop wish to expand their territories and there is a convenient river crossing in the area.

Berlin's origins lie in a merchant settlement established in the mid-12th century. A key travel route that led from southwest to northeast, from the Hellweg region to the Baltic Sea, across the River Spree close to what would later be known as Mühlendamm (Mill Dam), represents the spot at which the metropolis was founded. The first citizens settled on either side of the river, creating the twin towns of Berlin and Cölln. The impoundment of the Spree by at least one metre, which was implemented from Mühlendamm from the 13th century, made possible the operation of mills on the river and the Upper Spree navigable.

Cölln centred around St Peter's Church west of Mühlendamm, Berlin around St Nicholas' Church and St Mary's Church to the east of the Dam. On each side of Mühlendamm there was a fish market, a town hall, and the convent of a mendicant order – the Dominicans in Cölln, the Franciscans in Berlin. The three parish churches are examples of the late medieval model of hall church with an ambulatory. St Nicholas' and St Mary's still stand today, while on the site of St Peter's – which was repeatedly destroyed and rebuilt – the House of One is currently under construction, a communal building for all three of the Abrahamitical religions of the book.

This twin town was not simply two independent towns existing next to and in competition with each other. From the start, both towns were enclosed by a common city wall, of which remnants can still be seen on Waisenstraße. The city gates have since disappeared from the city's geography, but the squares to which they gave access still exist: Holzmarkt, Spittelmarkt, Hackescher Markt, and Alexanderplatz.

The evident trans-regional importance of the twin town in the 15th century piqued the interest of the new sovereigns from the House of Hohenzollern. They chose Berlin-Cölln as one of their residences and erected a castle in the northern quarter of Cölln – from then on into the 19th century the citizens had no say in their own city. Berlin remained encircled by its medieval walls well into the 17th century.

The Thirty Years' War was devastating for Berlin, but after its conclusion in 1648 the city gained prominence as the capital city of a rising, medium-sized European power. The militarily and economically successful reign of the Great Elector enabled the extension and embellishment of the residential palace from the 1660s onwards. New districts were established in the west of the city, which gradually developed into locations for satellite institutions associated with the princely court, such as the Zeughaus (Armory), the Opera, and the Academy of the Arts and Sciences.

Between 1658 and 1683 earthwork fortifications were erected around Berlin, Cölln, and the two small, new districts of Neukölln am Wasser and Friedrichswerder. These fortifications were razed after only sixty years, in the 1730s, but traces of their existence are still visible in the city layout.

In 1701 the Elector of Brandenburg gained royal status and became King in Prussia. This new status was given expression through architectural improvements to the residential city. The renaissance palace, which had replaced the 15th-century castle, made way for the Baroque structure of the Berlin Palace, designed by Andreas Schlüter, Eosander von Göthe, and Martin Heinrich Böhme. With the Baroque Zeughaus and the palace, Berlin now had representative buildings with which it could compete on the European stage. Over the nearly 250 years from the completion of the Berlin Palace in 1713 to its razing in 1951, the palace was the most important historical architectural structure of the city.

Between 1663 and 1740, 60 town houses for the nobility were constructed, which made a significant contribution to the beautification of the city. The architects were guided by architectural models in Italy, France, and Holland. At the start of the 18th century, Berlin was held in high regard as a Modern Baroque residence, outshining even Dresden and Munich.

This brief survey of the architectural development of historical Berlin demonstrates that the city was a *late bloomer* and developed *slowly, but prodigiously*. The relatively late onset in Italy and Germany of processes of national unification and industrialisation – compared with those of England and France – allowed Berlin to experience markedly accelerated growth in size and importance.

* Benedikt Goebel is Lecturer in Urban History and coordinator of the project Stadtkern in Berlin.

Berlin urban planning as a laboratory of ideas 1710-1989

Silvia Malcovati*

In January, 1710, Frederick I of Prussia decreed that the five royal residences of Berlin, Cölln, Friedrichswerder, Dorotheenstadt and Friedrichstadt would be combined under a single administration to form the capital of Berlin. The city became a young capital in rapid expansion, based on a process, in many ways exemplary: various planning strategies followed one another to create almost a user manual for urban planning.

West of the medieval city, the first expansion projects followed the principles of Baroque town layouts to the letter: straight roads intersected at right angles to form regular blocks, majestic squares, and representational units defining urban space. In this context, in the early 18th century, the Unter den Linden was built as the East-West axis, the western end being inaugurated in 1791 with the Brandenburg Gate. Friedrichstraße ran in the North-South direction, and the famous Pariser, Leipziger and Belle-Alliance Platz, based on the squares or "places" of Paris, were connected by the diagonal Wilhelmstraße. Even after destruction and reconstruction, this configuration still represents the skeleton layout of the centre of Berlin today.

Around 1800, Berlin had a population of 170,000, and covered a surface of 13.3 square kilometres; the perimeter was formed by the customs and excise wall that had replaced the fortifications. To close the gap between the Medieval and Baroque centres, K.F. Schinkel designed a Neoclassical centre, building isolated constructions with very precise dimensions and a strict architectural style, like the Neue Wache, the Schauspielhaus, Friedrichswerder church, Altes Museum and the Bauakademie, revolutionizing the Baroque style and redefining the urban hierarchies of the city centre. Together with the works of Peter Joseph Lenné, that consolidated the landscaping of the city, redesigning parks and creating new districts, still today, these interventions bear witness to a diversified structure characterised by the urban layouts and monumental constructions merged with nature.

From 1861, with the integration of various suburbs and agricultural areas from surrounding towns, the urban area reached 59 square kilometres, with a population of 550,000. Like all European capitals on the brink of the Industrial Revolution, the rapid increase in population brought the inevitable deterioration in living and hygiene conditions, so Berlin drew up a plan for urban expansion. The Hobrecht plan (1862) was based on roadway alignment, designed as a technical instrument to provide the city with an efficient canal system (still in existence), sustainable traffic circulation and modern infrastructures (like the railway and metropolitan systems which are still part of the Berlin urban layout).

This project was built according to a fifty year controlled expansion plan. The degeneration of this model (large city blocks, six storey buildings with internal courtyards with a minimum area of 5.34 square metres) combined with property speculation, led Werner Hegemann to describe Berlin as "the biggest rental barracks in the world" (1930). This opinion was already shared by his contemporaries and was to have radical consequences even in the post-war period.

At the beginning of the 20th century, Germany was the cradle of modern urban planning and the "Great Berlin" competition (1908-10) led to the introduction of advanced concepts incorporating mobility, landscaping and urban development for a metropolis with a (potential?) population of 10 million. (The joint winners were H. Jansen and Brix & Genzmer). The innovative expansion model with radial infrastructures and concentric circles continues to represent the heritage of those projects.

In 1920, a law was passed to ratify the unification of Berlin with surrounding suburbs. The city covered a surface of 878 square kilometres with a population of 3.8 million. It represented the most advanced laboratory on contemporary topics of metropolitan development and mass housing. Alongside alternative proposals for garden cities and experiments for reformed city blocks, the Modern/Modernist urban settlements of the Weimar Republic designed by some of the most famous architects of the period, are a reflection of the political, cultural and technical progress that occurred in the capital, and a fundamental chapter in the history of public housing. (Falkenberg, Schillerpark, Britz, Onkel Toms Hütte, Siemensstadt and Weiße Stadt were included among the UNESCO heritage sites in 2008).

Few traces remain of the plans for Berlin during the National Socialist period, mainly plans on paper, like the monumental North-South axis designed by A. Speer, while the city suffered dramatic consequences from war bombing. At the end of the war, Berlin was a city destroyed and then divided. It became an experimental field par excellence for modern urban planning. In both the East and West, though with different ideologies, there was same urgent desire to demonstrate renewal and progress. They demolished existing buildings, and inside and outside the historical centre they built a city focussed on automobile circulation. The Stalinallee (today, Karl-Marx-Allee, built in 1951) and the Hansa Viertel (1957) are the prime examples.

It was only in the mid-1970s that a reaction against this systematic destruction policy began to emerge among the public, architecture and government. This led to setting up the IBA in West Berlin (1984-87).

Shortly before reunification, the IBA focussed strongly on the topic of historic remains, urban blocks, and traditional housing styles. Through concepts such as "careful urban renewal" and "critical reconstruction" they were able to open the road to post-wall discussions in 1989.

* Silvia Malcovati is Architect and Professor of Architectural Composition at the Potsdam School of Architecture.

Berlin after 1989

Bernd Albers*

Not only was the division of Europe and of Germany ended with the fall of the Wall in 1989 and the unification of Germany in 1990, so was the division of Berlin. This called into question the idea of the twin city of Berlin, which had been cultivated ever since 1945 and especially since 1961, and had consequently penetrated deep into the subconsciousness of Berliners. "Berlin is many cities" became a key statement in the architectural and town planning debates of the period, even though all involved were well aware that the urban history of Berlin had grown out of a single historical centre. The joining of the city's East and West from 1990 onwards represented the completion of a tremendous human, administrative, and political effort that had significant consequences for the very idea of the city and thus impact on the development of Berlin to this day.

While the West Berlin city society was satisfied and generally happy with its focus on the western city centre around Breitscheidplatz and Kurfürstendamm, the East Berliners could look with pride to their historic centre and the urban expansions with the historic boundaries. At the same time, West Berliners became aware of the significance of the socialist refashioning of the city centre: the demolition of the old town, the erection of the Television Tower, the Palace of the Republic, and the GDR government buildings in the surrounding area.

Very quickly, the unexpected and rapid decision of the German Bundestag in June 1991 to make Berlin the seat of parliament and government brought decisive new impulses. It introduced a new momentum to the city development debates in Berlin, which would subsequently have a strong, stimulating influence on the commonalities of the two halves of the city. Henceforth, the debate was not simply about the reunification of the city of Berlin; instead, a reunited Germany was to have its capital in this city of Berlin. It goes without saying that this would call into question the results of socialist politics and its architects just as much as the products of national socialist architecture from 1933 to 1945. Yet, at the same time, the imperial structures also had to be reactivated anew and enduringly for the new cultural and political capital city.

In the city planning developments of this period the large-scale architectural competitions focusing on Potsdamer Platz and Leipziger Platz in 1991 (Hilmer, Sattler & Albrecht) and on Alexanderplatz in 1993 (Kollhoff + Timmermann) play a prominent role in the new dynamism and centrality of the Berlin city centre. Similarly, the 1992 competition for the river bend of the Spree (Schultes + Frank) on which the seat of parliament and government lies, as well as the 1994 competition (Niehbur) for the Spree Island – and thus the historical city centre – held extraordinary significance for the medium-term perspectives of the city. The East-West struggle within Berlin continued to simmer beneath the surface in this period, but was in general reduced to economic issues.

14

As the city transformed, so politics naturally gained a new importance. In 1991 the urban planning expert and Berlin connoisseur Hans Stimmann was given the office of Senate Director of Municipal Planning and Building Control and remained in this and related offices until 2006. Important decisions were made in this period, which were in no small part due to Stimmann's cultural attitude and strategic position with regard to the development of city planning. The revival of the historical city layout, the reactivation of the notion of property, especially in the eastern part of the city, the expansion of social, transport, and education infrastructures, and reflection of the qualities of traditional city architecture are certainly the result of his influence. In 1996 he began the city planning project Planwerk Innenstadt, which, over three years until 1999 cooperated with two teams (Ortner + Neumeyer in the West and Albers + Hoffmann-Axthelm in the East) to develop a plan for the Berlin city centre. The plan was approved by the Berlin senate after heated debates In May 1999 and has formed the basis for the urban strategy developments of Berlin ever since.

With the launch of the federal government in 1999, the international role of Berlin is increasingly underscored and tangible. The governmental buildings on the bend of the River Spree represent a fulcrum for the urban development of Berlin; the monumental cultural buildings on the Museum Island and its surroundings wield a growing influence on the cultural climate of the entire city and beyond. The decision of the German parliament in 2008 to approve the partial reconstruction of the city palace as the Humboldt-Forum (Stella) — which opened its doors in 2021 — means the historical centre of Berlin is once again characterised by a magnificent expression of Prussian Baroque palace architecture.

Only the areas around the Television Tower, along Grunerstraße, and around Alexanderplatz still seem to exist in limbo. They continue to convey an impression of the late functionalist and socialist inner city with its monumental roads and frequently over-dimensioned buildings — especially towards the East along Karl-Marx-Allee. Here time seems to have frozen, the old political positions entrenched and awaiting new impulses.

* Bernd Albers is Architect and Professor of Architecture and Construction at Potsdam School of Architecture.

Strategies for visiting Berlin

Visitors should approach Berlin with an open mind, aware that each place they visit will be different. Berlin is a city of layers, constantly undergoing change, difficult to interpret or classify unless it is perceived as an organic substance that has been torn apart, decorticated, and regenerated through every stage in history. It is eclectic, avant-garde, with architecture from late Baroque to formal Modern, a city built of heavy stone and transparent façades. East Berlin, West Berlin, and the interval between. The itineraries are grouped geographically to view an architecture that narrates layers of deep meaning, allowing the visitor to explore in a critical way, a city of coexistence that has been often uneasy.

Itinerary A / Museumsinsel – Friedrichstraße
This itinerary straddles the Museumsinsel and the long backbone of Friedrichstraße, part of the more widespread Mitte quarter, the historical centre of the former East Berlin. Within a short distance, it is easy to visit **Museumsinsel/01** specifically designed to group the main museums: the Altes Museum, the Bode, **Neues/02**, Pergamon and the **James-Simon-Galerie/03**, as well as the other cultural institutions built around the island, like the main Library, **Jacob-und-Wilhelm-Grimm-Zentrum/16**. Friedrichstraße is the connecting axis that crosses the city from north to south. It was built in the 18th century, badly bombed during the Second World War, and was the line along which the Berlin Wall was built. This section of the city is a perfect example of the extreme complexity of Berlin, its reconstructions and the traces of its past. Only a few metres apart, Checkpoint Charlie coexists with the large department stores designed by contemporary starchitects: **Galeries Lafayette/14** by Jean Nouvel, the different stores in the **Friedrichstadt-Passagen** by Ungers and Pei, and the completely rebuilt urban blocks like the Quartier Schützenstraße designed by Aldo Rossi.

Itinerary B / North Mitte
Mitte is a dynamic vibrant quarter, north of the River Spree, known for its experimental architecture from the early 20th century to the present day. In the same area are housing complexes by Bruno Taut, the **Haus Lemke/27** home by Mies van der Rohe, the reconstruction of the air raid bunker, **Dachgarten Sammlung Boros/18**, the tall and narrow **Slender-Bender/33** built at the start of the millennium, the **Velodrom/26** by Dominique Perrault, and the innovative Museum of the Future, **Futurium Berlin/34**.

Itinerary C / Mitte – Tiergarten
Moving slightly westward, this itinerary includes austere but extremely interesting architecture, beginning with the government administration quarter: the **Reichstag/36**, with its panoramic promenade under the glass dome designed by Foster and Partners, the Federal Chancellery, and the recent

innovative **cube berlin/40**, by 3XN, plus the intervention for the fire and police station that raised Sauerbruch Hutton's reputation to international status. The route continues towards Charlottenburg and Moabit with the impressive **AEG Turbinenhalle/44** by Peter Behrens and the futuristic **ICC/47** congress centre. The itinerary concludes in the south with the Tiergarten Park, home to a number of embassies, the Hansaviertel residential quarter designed by the masters of Modern architecture, and the **Kulturforum/62**, the cultural centre built for West Berlin.

Itinerary D / New Centre

This route takes visitors from west to east to view the reconstructions built around **Potsdamer Platz/70**, a "non-place" during the years of separation, but now the symbol of the new Berlin. The masterplan, designed by Renzo Piano, is amplified with excellent examples of contemporary architecture like the Kollhoff Tower, the **DZ Bank/67** by Frank Ghery, the **SONY Center/65** by Helmut Jahn, the moving Memorial to the murdered **Memorial to the Murdered Jews of Europe/66** by Peter Eisenman, and the **Library of the Freie Universität/74** by Foster.

Itinerary E / Friedrichshain – Kreuzberg

The last itinerary is focused on the Friedrichshain – Kreuzberg district; the first, renowned for a young and fairly homogeneous population (East Berlin) and the second for the large number of older and foreign inhabitants (West Berlin). This division was marginally addressed at the international architectural exhibition, "IBA 84", in an attempt to launch the difficult reconstruction and restoration of the more derelict buildings by introducing participatory project design and recalling traditional urban structure. One example is the famous **Bonjour Tristesse/84** by Álvaro Siza, or the older **Hufeisensiedlung/85** designed by Bruno Taut, that preceded the revision of the German housing model by several decades. The itinerary closes at the southern end of Friedrichstraße, with a visit to the **Jewish Museum/75** by Libeskind and the **Embassy of the Netherlands/77** by OMA.

2

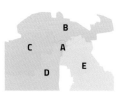

Routes

A. Museumsinsel –
Friedrichstraße
B. North Mitte
C. Mitte – Tiergarten
D. New Centre
E. Friedrichshain –
Kreuzberg

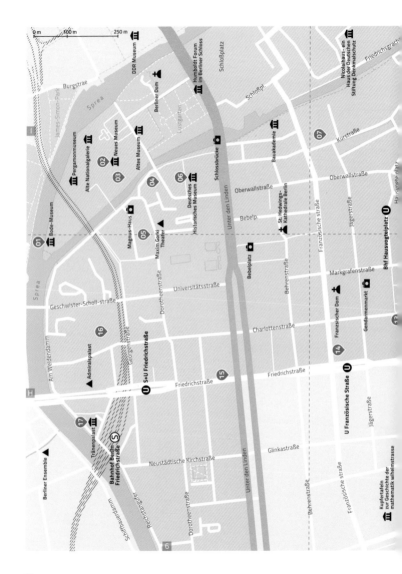

Museumsinsel –
Friedrichstraße

01. Museumsinsel
02. Museumsinsel –
    Neues Museum
03. Museumsinsel –
    James-Simon-Galerie
04. Haus Bastian
05. Collegium Hungaricum Berlin
06. Deutsches Historisches
    Museum (extension)
07. Reichsbank for the Ministry
    of Foreign Affairs
    (restoration)
08. Axel Springer Neubau
09. W. Michael Blumenthal
    Akademie
10. GSW Headquarters
    (extension)
11. Quartier Schützenstraße
12. Friedrichstadt-Passagen
    (Quartier 205)
13. Newton Bar
14. Galeries Lafayette
15. Friedrichstadt-Passagen
    (Quartier 206)
16. Jacob-und-Wilhelm-
    Grimm-Zentrum
17. Tränenpalast (Border
    Experiences) (installation)

01. Museumsinsel

Am Kupfergraben
10178 Berlin

Tue - Wed, Fri - Sun /
10 am - 6 pm
Thu / 10 am - 8 pm
Alte Nationalgalerie, Altes
Museum, Bode-Museum
Mon / closed

 U6 > Bahnhof Berlin
Friedrichstraße

 S3 / S5 / S7 / S9
> Bahnhof Berlin
Hackescher Markt

 100 / 245 / 300 >
Lustgarten

 12 / M1 >
Georgenstraße/Am
Kupfergraben

Museumsinsel is the most ambitious cultural project ever created by any public administration. It is composed of an island in the northern section of the River Spree, dedicated to the museums and cultural aspects of the city. The project was named a UNESCO heritage site in 1999, and was created in answer to the desire to build a renewed artistic heritage narrative aguard spirit of the city, during the largely radical period in 1989 with the fall of the Berlin Wall. In 1993, this spirit of renewal led to the launching of an international competition to design an entire masterplan for what was known as the Orangerie of Frederick William I of Brandenburg, a series of Italian style gardens and conservatories, later converted by Frederick I of Prussia into ancient art museums. The first building, and first public museum, was the Altes (Old) Museum inaugurated in 1830, designed by Friedrich Schinkel. The Neoclassical style museum directly overlooks the Lustgarten and its entrance forms a fine division between the classical collection exhibitions and the rest of the buildings. Behind it are the Alte Nationalgalerie, the Neues Museum, and the Bode-Museum, the last building that forms the rounded profile of the end of the island, plus, plus the Pergamonmuseum whose northern wing housed the Deutsche Museum now in the Zeughaus Baroque armoury, on the other side of the canal restored by Pei. Although each building belongs to a different period, the complex

architects
Karl Friedrich Schinkel (Altes Museum), Friedrich August Stüler (Alte Nationalgalerie), Ernst Eberhard von Ihne (Bode-Museum), Alfred Messel, Ludwig Hoffmann (Pergamonmuseum)

type
museum complex

construction
1830 (Altes Museum), 1876 (Alte Nationalgalerie), 1904 (Bode-Museum), 1910-1930 (Pergamonmuseum)

stands out because of the unifying design of the connecting routes, known as the Archaeological Promenade. The project, designed by David Chipperfield Architects, already existed in a different form during the initial constructions in 1843, with bridges and raised walkways. A new underground passageway forms a backbone that connects the museums, creating a continuous reading of all the collections on show in the various institutions, beginning with the James-Simon-Galerie that forms the unique entrance. The route includes nine zones with different themes and conducts the viewing sequence, guiding and underlining the specific nature of each collection: "Portrait and Concept of the Human being", "God and the Gods", "Order of the World", "Time and History", "Voyage into the Afterlife", "Place and Refuge", "Ornamentation and Abstraction", "Communication and Transport" and "The Art of Memory".

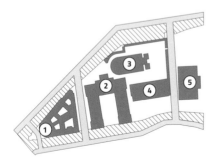

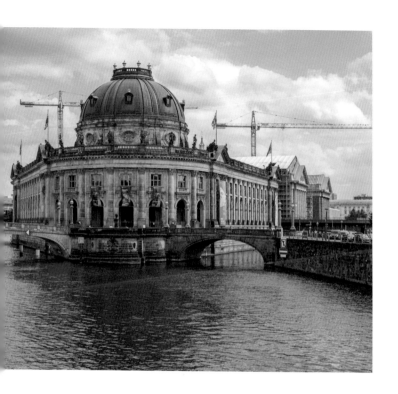

1. Bode-Museum
2. Pergamonmuseum
3. Alte Nationalgalerie
4. Neues Museum
5. Altes Museum

02. Museumsinsel – Neues Museum

Bodestraße 1-3
10178 Berlin

Tue - Sun / 10 am - 6 pm

+49 (0) 30 266 424 242
service@smb.museum
www.smb.museum

 U6 > Bahnhof Berlin Friedrichstraße

 S3 / S5 / S7 / S9 > Bahnhof Berlin Hackescher Markt

 100 / 245 / 300 > Lustgarten

 12 / M1 > Georgenstraße/Am Kupfergraben

This project, part of the State Museum complex on the Museum Island, won the Mies van der Rohe Prize in 2011. The original museum was built between 1841 and 1859 by Stüler, who studied under Schinkel, but it suffered irreparable damage during the Second World War, and was left untouched until 1986. The restoration project was assigned to the English firm, David Chipperfield Architects, which followed the guidelines of the Charter of Venice, drawn up in 1964, for respecting conservation and restoration methods in historical heritage buildings. The project respects the historical structure in its different states of preservation, blending the ruins with new interventions: a subtle fusion of the various layers where the new elements reflect the missing parts of the building without imitating them. The reconstruction has created a new traffic flow system more appropriate to contemporary requirements, with the introduction of a spacious foyer that contains a bookshop, ticket office, and lockers. It also includes the majestic staircase made from white cement mixed with Saxonian marble chips. The internal layout and graphics were created by the Milanese firm, Michele de Lucchi, with a series of specifically built support bases, display cases and pedestals designed to intensify the visitor's viewing pleasure without dominating the artworks.

 © David Chipperfield Architects

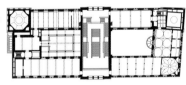

architects
Friedrich August Stüler /
David Chipperfield Architects,
AMDL CIRCLE (staging and
graphic design)

type
museum

construction
1855 / 2003-2009

03. Museumsinsel – James-Simon-Galerie

Bodestraße
10178 Berlin

Mon - Sun /
9.30 am - 6.30 pm

+49 (0) 30 266 424 242
service@smb.museum
www.smb.museum

 U6 > Berlin
Friedrichstraße station

 S3 / S5 / S7 / S9
> Bahnhof Berlin
Hackescher Markt

 100 / 245 / 300 >
Lustgarten

 12 / M1 >
Georgenstraße/Am
Kupfergraben

With the Archaeological Promenade, the James-Simon-Galerie, named after the great art patron, forms the new entrance to the state museum complex on the Museum Island. This innovative element provides an unusual view of the relationships and proportions among urban systems, by placing a clean parallelepiped structure on a podium raised above street level. Like the Neue Nationalgalerie, the space assumes the role of the archetypal Greek public square for interrelation and cross passage, a public space that links culture and urban life. The access staircases are enclosed within the propylaea gateway that reestablishes the profile of the narrow site that once housed the customs warehouse; the base plinth rises above the water providing unique views through the large openings overlooking the canal. The relationship with the overall context continues internally: the main routes converge in the central foyer with views over the river, especially on the lower level. The walls are built using vast slabs of smoothed concrete with some areas clad in wood; the foyer contains a bistro restaurant, ticket office, and auditorium.

© David Chipperfield Architects

architects
David Chipperfield Architects

type
visitor centre

construction
2019

04. Haus Bastian

Am Kupfergraben 10
10117 Berlin

open to the public
by appointment

+49 (0) 30 831 6001
info@bastian-gallery.com
www.bastian-gallery.com

 U6 > Berlin
Friedrichstraße station

 S3 / S5 / S7 / S9
> Bahnhof Berlin
Hackescher Markt

 100 / 245 / 300 >
Lustgarten

 12 / M1 >
Georgenstraße/Am
Kupfergraben

Haus Bastian is a gallery that overlooks the Kupfergraben canal, opposite the Museum Island and the newly completed James-Simon-Galerie. The project won the competition launched by the previous owners who donated the building to the Berlin Municipality in 2019 for use as a cultural and educational centre. The building is a contemporary reinterpretation of the adjacent historical architectural context, and closes the façade of a site destroyed by war bombing. The parallelepiped structure is attached on two sides to historic buildings from the late Wilhelminian period, replicating the height but not the style. The result is a sculptural block with large recessed openings with loggias and wood-framed windows in contrast with the light coloured stone of the façade. The interior is cleverly proportioned and flooded with natural daylight from the large windows. The four floors intersect around a central light well that connects the various functional spaces of the building.

architects
David Chipperfield Architects

type
art gallery

construction
2007

05. Collegium Hungaricum Berlin

Dorotheenstraße 12
10117 Berlin

Mon - Fri / 1 pm - 6 pm

+49 (0) 30 21 23 400
collegium@hungaricum.de
www.berlin.balassiintezet.hu

 U6 > Berlin
Friedrichstraße station

 S3 / S5 / S7 / S9
> Bahnhof Berlin
Hackescher Markt

 100 / 245 / 300 >
Staatsoper

 12 / M1 >
Georgenstraße/Am
Kupfergraben

The Collegium Hungaricum Berlin was erected on the former site of the first Hungarian Cultural Institute, and shows a clear reference to Bauhaus Modernism. The pristine, white, six-floor building houses guest apartments, a library, seminar rooms, and the Moholy-Nagy gallery. The pure white building features large windows with contrasting black frames with views of the surrounding landscape. The linear profile of the parallelepiped structure is interrupted by a loggia that echoes the corner entrance with its cantilevered roof. The heart of the building is the glassed-in panorama room that overlooks the central plaza like a huge aquarium. It is used for lectures, conferences, concerts, film screenings, informal meetings and special events.

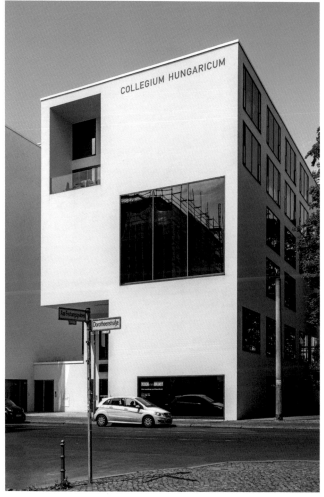

architects
Schweger Associated
Architects

type
cultural centre

construction
2014

06. Deutsches Historisches Museum (extension)

Unter den Linden 2
10117 Berlin

10 am - 6 pm
Thu / 10 am - 8 pm

+49 (0) 30 203 040
info@dhm.de
www.dhm.de

 U6 > Französische
Straße

 S3 / S5 / S7 / S9
> Bahnhof Berlin
Hackescher Markt

 100 / 245 / 300 >
Staatsoper

 12 / M1 >
Georgenstraße/Am
Kupfergraben

The project for the German History Museum has a complex past that dates back to the 1950s. The competition was originally won by Aldo Rossi, but after the fall of the Berlin Wall, the commission was passed directly to Pei. Unlike the original project that involved a completely new building, the second version was composed of an extension to an 18th century building that housed a history museum in East Berlin. Pei's unusual design lies in the juxtaposition of two buildings to form a combined museum enriched with unconventional walkways and corridors that open out to the surrounding urban space. The sandstone exhibition rooms give greater impact to the narrative and the objects on display, while the connecting spaces play a leading role with changing glimpses of the urban landscape. The entirely glazed entrance foyer is a vast space with a ceiling four storeys high. The severe lines are softened by the circular glazed staircase positioned on the corner of the Unter den Linden and the Hinter dem Zeughaus, looking towards the River Spree. The internal colour scheme is very neutral, but different materials were used for variation: granite for the floors, limestone on the walls and concrete for the slab.

architects
Pei Cobb Freed & Partners

type
museum

construction
2003

07. Reichsbank for the Ministry of Foreign Affairs (restoration)

Werderscher Markt 1
10117 Berlin

Mon - Fri / 9 am - 3 pm

+49 (0) 30 18 170

www.auswaertiges-amt.de

 U2 > U Hausvogteiplatz

 147 > Werderscher Markt

The original building designed by Heinrich Wolff was built between 1934 and 1938, one of the few examples of Nazi architecture commissioned in 1933 with the launching of a competition that attracted numerous architects like Walter Gropius and Mies van der Rohe. It was initially designed to house the Reichsbank, but following the reunification of Germany, was annexed to the Ministry of Foreign Affairs complex that needed essential modifications to cater to its new functions. The restoration project was designed by Hans Kollhoff and involved the renovation of the internal layout to provide greater fluidity throughout, while preserving the original character of the building's façades. The project also included reinstating the structure of the main entrance that featured a steel framework, technically highly innovative for the 1930s, but which had been walled over during previous reconstruction work. The historical architecture was accentuated even further with the re-opening of the original skylights in corridors and offices, and the sequence of the various spaces was highlighted with the use of a monochromatic theme for interior walls designed in collaboration with the artist Gerhard Merz. The restoration incorporated planted terraces and gardens open to the public and employees in the building. It also included the transformation of the X-ray unit building into an independent house clad in green ceramic tiles.

architects	**type**	**construction**
Kollhoff Architekten	offices	2000

08. Axel Springer Neubau

Schützenstraße 26
10117 Berlin

partially open to the public

+49 (0) 30 25 91 77 601
information@axelspringer.de
www.axelspringer-neubau.de

 U2 / U6 > U
Spittelmarkt;
U Kochstraße/
Checkpoint Charlie

 200 / 265 / N2 >
Jerusalemer Straße
248 / M29 / N42 >
Lindenstraße/
Oranienstraße

The new building for the Axel Springer digital media company was designed by OMA, winning project in a competition including important participants like BIG and Büro Ole Scheeren. The building is bisected by a diagonal pedestrian atrium that defines the internal space of the building: the single block structure reveals its strength in the tall section over 30 metres high, along which a range of various functional areas are arranged in answer to company necessities, creating a continuous play of different perspectives throughout the building. The project interpreted the new 3.0 working requisites by designing the diagonal axis or "Valley" as the intersection for the different traffic flows. It is also linked to a series of terraces, aerial walkways at different heights, and other individual, team or mobile workspaces. The building becomes an active support for the company's functional and cultural activities, facilitating work method transformation and creating continuity between the internal space and the city, through the ground floor with its galleries, temporary exhibition and multi-function spaces and restaurants.

architects
OMA

type
offices

construction
2013-under construction

09. W. Michael Blumenthal Akademie

**Fromet-und-Moses-
Mendelssohn-Platz 1**
10969 Berlin

Tue - Thu / 12 am - 5 pm
Fri - Mon / closed

+49 (0) 30 25 99 33 00

www.jmberlin.de

**U6 / U1 / U3 / U6 /
U12** > U Kochstraße/
Checkpoint Charlie;
Hallesches Tor

248 / N42 >
Jüdisches Museum
M29 > Lindenstraße/
Oranienstraße

The W. Michael Blumenthal Akademie is located on the site of the former wholesale flower market in Fromet-und-Moses-Mendelssohn-Platz. Today it houses the association's archives and a library that is open to the public with educational and teaching activities. The project was based on *Zwischenräume*, or "in-between spaces". In a very unique manner, it forms a creative circuit that focuses on crevices, unresolved spaces, and thresholds that combine to create a fluid narrative among the various structural elements. Three tilting cubes intersect and embrace so that they penetrate one another completely. The first cube is newly built and forms the slanting entrance. It is clad in pine wood and is rooted in the site, sloping upwards until it joins the hall of the 'Old Building', or Kollegienhaus. Two other tilted buildings house the library and the auditorium. The unifying element in this formal maze is the Garden of Exile, a landscape of tall columns containing plants from all over the world, and a covered square with 360-degree views of all the buildings in the complex.

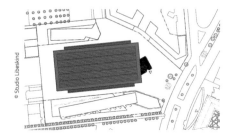

© Studio Libeskind

architects
Studio Libeskind

type
education

construction
2012

10. GSW Headquarters (extension)

Charlottenstraße 4
10969 Berlin

external viewing only

+49 (0) 30 68 99 990

www.deutsche-wohnen.com/gsw

U6 > U Kochstraße/
Checkpoint Charlie

M29 >
Charlottenstraße

This was the winning project in a competition launched in 1991 to expand the original structure built in the 1950s. It involved the rearranging of several urban fragments through the juxtaposition of five buildings to reflect both the Baroque and the 20th century morphology of this urban block, 250 metres from Checkpoint Charlie. The most distinctive element of the complex is the tallest building that runs along the west side of the area. Attached to the existing building is a double skin featuring a constantly changing façade of red, orange and pink sun shield panels, that become a milky white colour on the eastern side. On the other hand, the curved concave base structure is rooted to the ground, in contrast with the striking height of the other building, with a series of small-sized atriums and foyers. This is a vibrant and dynamic project because every façade absorbs, integrates and rearranges different urban elements through authentic layering and reinterpretation of the historic memory of the city. Some of the outstanding elements of this expansion project are the sustainable design techniques adopted, with integrated closure systems to provide natural cross-ventilation and facilitate air flow from east to west. The projecting aerodynamic wing roof on the tallest building is designed to prevent air pressure build-up of natural thermal currents.

© Sauerbruch Hutton

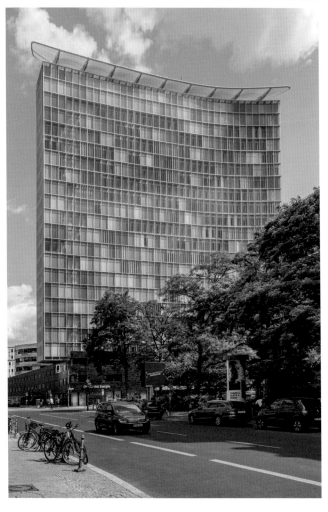

architects
Sauerbruch Hutton

type
offices

construction
1999

11. Quartier Schützenstraße

Charlottenstraße 16
10117 Berlin

partially open to the public

 U6 > U Kochstraße/
Checkpoint Charlie

 M29 >
Charlottenstraße

Quartier Schützenstraße is one of the most renowned complexes in the Mitte area. It was built shortly after the fall of the Berlin Wall as part of the urban reconstruction policy aimed at transforming this portion of the city to provide a renewed public image. Aldo Rossi designed the complex which is spread over a 70,000 square metre area, an entire city block that lies between Schützenstraße (north), Markgrafenstraße (east), Charlottenstraße (west) and along the line of the Zimmerstraße, the "Death Strip" of the former Berlin Wall that divided East and West Berlin. The complex is an example of Postmodern architecture, rich in classical elements from the Wilhelmine period, Italian Rationalism with Renaissance citations (explicit references to the Farnese Palace in Rome) all able to integrate with the pre-existent buildings through a reconstruction of the typical traditional Berlin model of the early 20th century. It is a city block with internal courtyards, bordered by four streets, and broken up into 12 sections with different styles, dimensions, forms, colours, building materials and technologies. The grey ground floor base is the only common element of each façade. The complex contains four internal courtyards designed as internal gardens that act as public passageways between one side of the city block to the other.

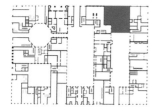

architects
Aldo Rossi, Bellman & Böhm

type
residential, offices

construction
1997

12. Friedrichstadt-Passagen (Quartier 205)

Friedrichstraße 67
10117 Berlino

Mon - Sat / 8 am - 10 pm

www.quartier-205.com

 **U2 / U6** > U Stadtmitte

Friedrichstadt-Passagen, better-known in Berlin as Quartier 205, is one of three large city blocks connected by underground walkways and retail stores. This single block covers 53,000 square metres and houses retail businesses, office spaces and residential apartments. The city block is composed of a massive building, in typical Berlin architectural style, that interacts with its context, not through contrast but by mitigating its presence, adapting its height to that of the adjacent six-floor buildings, rising to nine floors in the central body which encloses two internal courtyards. The architectural composition is based on a strict four square module, repeated on the façades clad in light-coloured stone, and the window frames, each divided into four squares. The same module is applied to the internal courtyard façades and the interior of the building, visible in the ceilings and glazed roofing. The foyer houses the sculpture *Der Turm von Klythie*, created by John Chamberlain in 1995. The building also hosts a temporary showing of two works by the American artist, Joel Shapiro.

architect
Oswald Mathias Ungers

type
retail, offices, residential

construction
1991-1995

13. Newton Bar

Charlottenstraße 57
10117 Berlin

Sun - Wed / 11 am - 3 am
Thu - Sat / 11 am - 4 am

+49 (0) 30 20 29 54 21
info@newton-bar.de
www.newton-bar.de

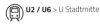 **U2 / U6** > U Stadtmitte

 N6 > U Stadtmitte

Located inside the Oscar Mathias Ungers building on Gendarmenmarkt, this project to renew the Newton Bar was designed to integrate harmoniously within a very complex urban fabric. According to the architect, Kollhoff: "It had to look as if it had always been here". The bar is named after the famous photographer whose Foundation is only a few metres away. It has a long mobile counter in solid palisander wood that can be extended out onto the side walk. The long interior is faced in green and white Cipollino marble and lacquered palisander panelling, leaving generous space for the leather seating. The walls are lined with mirrors to expand the sense of space, and feature original photographs by Helmut Newton. A spiral staircase set into the Cipollino marble leads to an upstairs space. This room has a warm welcoming atmosphere with a gilded ceiling and period printed wallpaper.

© Kollhoff Architekten

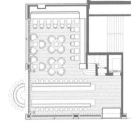

architects
Kollhoff Architekten

type
restaurant

construction
1999

14. Galeries Lafayette

Friedrichstraße 76-78
10117 Berlin

Mon - Sat / 10 am - 8 pm

+49 (0) 30 20 94 80

www.galerieslafayette.de

 U6 > Französische
Straße

 147 > Französische
Straße

Like most of the reconstruction projects along
Friedrichstraße, Galeries Lafayette occupy a
large portion of an entire city block. The project is the result of a competition launched in
1990; Jean Nouvel won the commission to
rebuild Lot 207 (for this reason the block is also
called Quartier 207). The building is designed as
a transparent encircling shell for product display: iridescent but opaque during the day, it is
lit up with advertising billboards at night. New
technology, using glass on both the façades
and the squared dome roof, reflects light inside
the building, creating strong impact through the
radiant visual continuity between exterior and
interior, between the horizontal areas and the
roof, in a constant play of changing perspectives. In fact, this is one of the most outstanding
elements of the project: ten monumental cones
and cylinders, composed of glass panels in different sizes set at different angles, create "irregular voids" that let in natural day light directly
from the roof dome through to the underground
floors, ten metres below street level.

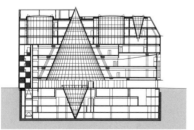

architects
Jean Nouvel, Emmanuel
Cattani & Associés

type
retail

construction
1996

15. Friedrichstadt-Passagen (Quartier 206)

Friedrichstraße
10117 Berlin

external viewing only

 U6 > Französische
Straße

 147 > Französische
Straße

The Quartier 206 is one of a series of major shopping centres built along the Friedrichstraße, connected with one another by underground corridors. The Quartier 206 building was designed to complete the urban block and features striking projecting elements that increase the vertical effect of the façades, contrasted by the horizontal bands in black and white marble, typical of 1920s Berlin architecture. The severe lines of the façade are repeated in the interior design, meticulously decorated with wall panels and mosaics in black, sienna, and sand coloured marble and stone. The string course lines are marked by rows of Art Déco style appliques, and the same theme is continued in the triple height main atrium that features a wide curving staircase. This space features a glass skylight with a sharply angular and irregular geometrical design supported by a white steel structure set on pillars that surround the whole triple height atrium. At night, the building glows with a geometrical play of light creating great impact.

architects
Pei Cobb Freed & Partners

type
retail

construction
1996

16. Jacob-und-Wilhelm-Grimm-Zentrum

Geschwister-Scholl-Straße 1-3
10117 Berlin

Mon - Fri / 9 am - 7 pm
Sat / 10 am - 6 pm

+49 (0) 30 20 93 99 370

www.hu-berlin.de

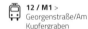

12 / M1 >
Georgenstraße/Am
Kupfergraben

The central library reflects the German tradition of great civic monumental architecture, proposing a contemporary version of a building for public use based on a close dialogue with the context. The towering mass rises like a vast sculpture over the Berlin skyline normally limited to a height of 22 metres. The library is 38 metres high, similar to other important monuments in the city, to underline its significant public function. The double-height ground floor interacts with the proportions of the other adjacent buildings and the height of the S-Bahn viaduct nearby, creating a continuum with the pedestrian zone. The dialogue between interior and exterior is defined by the very large reading hall, a central space with great impact, overlooked by smaller reading and study rooms, also linked with the exterior thanks to openings of various sizes in the façade. The interior is decorated with classical finishes in subdued colours like the grey and white surfaces and warm toned wood, in contrast with the façades clad in Treuchtlingen marble with light yellow veining.

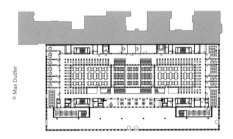

© Max Dudler

architect
Max Dudler

type
library

construction
2009

17. Tränenpalast (Border Experience) (installation)

Reichstagufer 17
10117 Berlin

Tue - Fri / 9 am - 7 pm
Sat - Sun / 9.30 am - 6 pm

+49 (0) 30 46 77 77 911
berlin@hdg.de
www.hdg.de/traenenpalast

 U6 > Berlin
Friedrichstraße station

 S1 / S2 / S5 / S7 / S25 / S75 > Berlin
Friedrichstraße station

 147 / N6 / RE1 / RE7
> Berlin Friedrichstraße
station

 12 / M1 > Berlin
Friedrichstraße station

The Tränenpalast, known as the "Palace of Tears", is the building that houses the permanent exhibition of the Site of German Division, formerly the control station between East and West Berlin. Today, as it did before, this elegant structure hides its true function: behind the well-lit glazed foyer, gracefully modelled with its staggered rectangular windows, are the oppressive inspection rooms. The Coordination project is focussed precisely on this duality: on one hand it leaves room for the historic reconstruction of the customs control, and on the other, the central foyer, with a route that guides visitors through the historic narrative. Each narrative station is marked by concrete structural elements to give greater impact, with dark panels that form a background for the display of many objects belonging to the people who passed in transit through the Tränenpalast.

© COORDINATION

architects
COORDINATION

type
museum

construction
2011

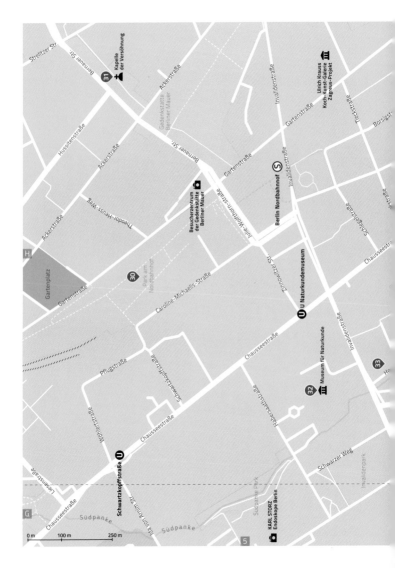

Kapelle
der Versöhnung

Strelitzer Str

Bernauer Str.

Hussitenstraße

Ackerstraße

Ackerstraße

Theodor-Heuss-Weg

Gedenkstätte Berliner Mauer

Ackerstraße

Bernauer Str.

Gartenplatz

H

Gartenstraße

Besucherzentrum
der Gedenkstätte
Berliner Mauer

Julie-Wollmann-straße

Gartenstraße

Invalidenstraße

Gartenstraße

Ulrich Krauss
Koch-Kunst-Galerie
Zagreus-Projekt

Teckstraße

Borsigst

Berlin Nordbahnhof Ⓢ

Invalidenstraße

Schlegelstraße

Chausseestr

Park am Nordbahnhof

Caroline-Michaelis-Straße

Zinnowitzer Str.

Ⓤ U Naturkundemuseum

Chausseestraße

Invalidenstraße

Lexisstraße

Chausseestraße

Pflugstraße

Schwartzkopffstraße

Schwarzkopffstraße

Wöhlertstraße

Chausseestraße

Museum für Naturkunde ⛪

Habersaathstraße

Invalidenpark

Schwarzer Weg

33

Ⓤ Schwartzkopffstraße

Südpanke

Tel von Arnim Str.

Südparke Park

Südpanke

KARL STORZ
Endoskope Berlin

G

0 m   100 m   250 m

5

B1

North Mite

18. Dachgarten Sammlung
Boros (renovation)
19. JOH3
20. Berlin Metropolitan
School (extension)
21. Hamburger Hof
22. Campus Joachimstraße
23. Tchoban Foundation –
Museum for Architectural
Drawing
24. Greifswalder Office Building
25. CB19

Schönhauser Alle Ⓢ Ⓤ

Ⓗumannplatz

✝ Gethsemanekirche

Wichertstraße

Schwedter Str.

Yestader Str.

Gleimstraße

Stargarder Str.

Gleimstraße

Falkplatz

Gaudystraße

Pappelallee

Stargarder Str.

Dunckerstraße

4

Graunstraße

Swinemünder Str.

Graunstraße

Buchholzer Str.

Raumerstraße

Helmholtzplatz

Zeiss-Gro

Demminer Str.

Wolliner Str.

Mauerpark

Pappelallee

Lychener Str.

Schliemannstraße

Raumerstraße

MACHmit!
Museum für Kinder 🏛
in Prenzlauer Berg

Ruppiner Str.

U Eberswalder
Str. (Berlin) Ⓤ

Bundesstraße 96a

Bernauer Str.

Museum in der 🏛
Kulturbrauerei

🏛 Plattenpalast

Oderberger Str.

KulturBrauerei 🏛

Husemannstraße

Sredzkistraße

Christbe

Ⓤ Bernauer Straße

Swinemünder Str.

Wollliner Str.

Schwedter Str.

Granseer Str.

Kastanienallee

Choriner Str.

Sredzkistraße

Schönhauser Alle

Wörther Str.

Kollwitzplatz

Jat

Brunnenstraße

Strelzer Str.

Fehrbelliner Str.

Zionskirchplatz

Zionskirchstraße

Schwedter Str.

☆ Synagoge
Rykestraße

Kollwitzstraße

Prenzlauer Allee

Veteranenstraße

Weinbergsweg

📷 Wasserturm

Museum 🏛
Pankow

Immanuelkirch

5

Invalidenstraße

Volkspark
am Weinberg

Choriner Str.

Fehrbelliner Str.

Ackerstraße

Brunnenstraße

Zehdenicker Str.

Lottumstraße

Schönhauser Allee

Ⓤ Senefelderplatz

Metzer Str.

Heinrich-Roller-straße

Leise-Park

Ⓤ Rosenthaler
Platz (Berlin) Ⓤ

Torstraße

Linienstraße

23
Tchoban 🏛
Foundation

Straßburger Str.

Saarbrücker Str.

Prenzlauer Allee

Torstraße

🏛 Fenster61

🏛 Ag Friedhofsmuseum
Berlin Ev

Torstraße

Rosenthaler Str.

22

Augustraße

Gipsstraße

🏛 KW Institute for
Contemporary Art

Gormannstraße

Mulackstraße

Ⓤ Rosa-Luxemburg-Platz Ⓤ

Schendelpark

Linienstraße

Torstraße

Prenzlauer Berg

Mausoleum der 🏛
Familie Brose

Oder-Braun-Straße

✝ Sophienkirche

21

Almstadtstraße

▲ Volksbühne

Mollstraße

6

🏛 Photogalerie
Oranienburger Straße

Ⓤ Weinmeisterstraße

Karl-Liebknecht-Str.

Wadzeckstraße

Ehemaliges Berliner
Frauengefängnis

Mollstraße

J

1

0 m   200 m   500 m

B2

North Mitte

26. Velodrom and Schwimm-
    und Sprunghalle im
    Europasportpark
27. Haus Lemke
28. Wohnstadt Carl Legien
29. Terrassenhaus Berlin
30. Park am Nordbahnhof
31. Kapelle der Versöhnung
32. Museum für Naturkunde
    (extension)
33. Slender-Bender
34. Futurium Berlin
35. Marie-Elisabeth-Lüders-
    Haus and Paul-Löbe-Haus

18. Dachgarten Sammlung Boros (renovation)

Reinhardtstraße 20
10117 Berlin

Thu / 3 pm - 6 pm
Fri - Sun / 10 am - 6 pm
open to the public
by appointment

+49 (0) 30 27 59 40 65
info@sammlung-boros.de
www.sammlung-boros.de

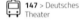 **147** > Deutsches
Theater

On the corner of Reinhardtstraße and Albre-chtstraße is a massive building that houses one of the most important private collections of contemporary art from 1990 to the present date. Since 2008, the collector Christian Boros and his family have lived on the top floor of the five-storey building, which was once was a Nazi bunker, built in 1943 by Karl Bonatz as an air raid shelter to hold up to 3,000 people. Over the years it has had many functions, from a storage warehouse for tropical fruit (earning it the name "Banana Bunker"), to a space for rave and fetish parties, until its closure in 1995. Today the building has been renovated to house 700 works of art that are displayed in rotation throughout the 80 rooms of the gallery. The reconstruction project by Realarchitektur was based on subtraction: 750 cubic metres of concrete were hand sawn and removed using a diamond cutting process to eliminate layers accumulated over time, while the internal walls and traces of dirt, blood and neon were left intact. The heights of certain rooms were adapted according to the exhibition function, raising ceilings from the original 2,30 metres to give greater impact for the viewing experience.

architects
Karl Bonatz, Realarchitektur

type
exhibition

construction
2008

19. JOH3

Johannistraße 3
10117 Berlin

external viewing only

 U6 > Oranienburger Tor

 S1 / S2 / S25 / S26 >
Oranienburger Straße

M1 / M5 >
Oranienburger Straße

The JOH3 project is a reinterpretation of the traditional Berlin residential blocks with apartments overlooking internal courtyards. This building creates an ambivalent relationship in the urban fabric: extrovertive in its formal contact with the city, because of the façade's suspended slat cladding that creates a fluid landscape between solid and void surfaces, and introvertive, where the private apartments overlook the internal garden. The south-west layout of the courtyard imposed the enforced rotation of the apartments facing the garden, making each residence different and with a dynamic style. Each apartment has a different size and layout: town-houses with private gardens as well as classic apartments or penthouses. The building's most unusual feature is the suspended slatted façade that creates a sinuous effect both internally and on the exterior.

© J. MAYER H. und Partner

architects
J. MAYER H. und Partner

type
residential

construction
2012

20. Berlin Metropolitan School (extension)

Linienstraße 122
10115 Berlin

partially open to the public

+49 (0) 30 88 72 73 90
info@metropolitanschool.com
www.metropolitanschool.com

 **U6** > Oranienburger Tor

The extension to this famous school, built in the 1980s, was focused on placing four prefabricated parallelepiped sections on the roofs of the existing building, plus an annex next to the main entrance, also clad in copper sheeting. The top floors of the existing structure were extended to house new music rooms, green planted terraces, and a new auditorium, built in warm coloured materials and designed to increase natural light. The construction plan had to focus on a structure that was easy to assemble on site without interrupting school lessons. The architects chose a prefabricated wooden skeleton frame covered with copper panels that reflect the warm colours of the existing brick building, while underlining the contrast in materials at the same time.

M1 / M5 >
Oranienburger Tor

© Sauerbruch Hutton

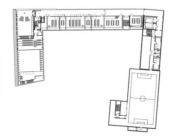

architects
Sauerbruch Hutton

type
education

construction
2019

21. Hamburger Hof

Grosse Hamburger Straße 17
10115 Berlin

external viewing only

hello@hamburgerhof.net
www.hamburgerhof.net

M1 / M5 >
Monbijouplatz

This redevelopment project is part of a complex of buildings, 200 years old, that have undergone several extensions and modifications to house a wide range of activities like a bowling club, a bronze casting workshop, a coffee roastery, a hardware store, a brewery, restaurants and bars in the past, and a combination of residential and small office units today. The new structure interprets the business and housing mix in a contemporary light, reinforcing the community atmosphere and functional destination of the complex through the juxtaposition of a new vertical structure built against a blind wall, and the reconstruction of attic spaces, destroyed during the Second World War. This composition guarantees the intimate feeling of the internal courtyard and accentuates its urban aspect with different façades that overlook the neighbourhood and nearby parks. The result is a complex where old brick buildings form a deliberately contrast with the contemporary steel-clad structures, in a play between the cantilevered elements projecting over the internal courtyard and the large vertical windows that vary the relationship between inside and out.

© TCHOBAN VOSS Architekten

architects
TCHOBAN VOSS Architekten

type
creative centre, residential

construction
2010

22. Campus Joachimstraße

Joachimstraße 11
10119 Berlin

open to the public

+49 (0) 30 28 01 700

 U8 > U Rosenthaler
Platz

 142 / N8 / N40 >
U Rosenthaler Platz

M1 / M8 >
U Rosenthaler Platz

This Campus project reinterprets the morphology of a city block fragment, in the form of a sharp slice, wedged between the buildings of a former piano factory. The project is composed of a series of buildings and garden spaces. The façade structure forms a barrier between the street and the internal courtyard, and is attached to the existing adjacent buildings, while two vertical blocks highlight the entrance to the internal urban space. A fourth building closes the composition. The first building is an exhibition space for temporary showings and events, and also includes an apartment, while the two internal buildings house student lodgings, university offices and a canteen which creates a link between the interior and the garden spaces designed by Peter Wirtz, for meeting and socialising. The monolithic reinforced concrete walls feature large square flush windows and form the main architectural focus in a contrasting dialogue with the pre-existent buildings. The interiors have very plain finishes: polished concrete floors, hand painted panels for doors and fixtures, and veined marble slabs for bathrooms and kitchens.

© David Chipperfield Architects

architects
David Chipperfield Architects

type
offices

construction
2013

23. Tchoban Foundation – Museum for Architectural Drawing

Christinenstrasse 18a
10119 Berlin

Mon - Fri / 2 pm - 7 pm
Sat - Sun / 1 pm - 5 pm

+49 (0) 30 43 73 90 90
mail@tchoban-foundation.de
www.tchoban-foundation.de

 **U2** > U Senefelderplatz

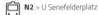 **N2** > U Senefelderplatz

The area where the Tchoban Foundation is built was developed in the 1990s to create a zone for the Berlin artistic and cultural scene; it is home to many workshops, art studios and artists apartments, creative agencies and galleries. The museum houses Sergei Tchoban's personal collection of architectural drawings, that include rare and refined drawings dating between the 16th and 21st centuries, and also hosts rotating temporary exhibitions. The building makes a strong statement overlooking the public square in front, where the various façades show the different etching processes used on the concrete cubes. This includes relief engravings that provide a hint of the museum content. Despite the blind façades, the irregularly off-set, sand-coloured blocks, with their etched decoration, have an extremely dynamic, lightweight effect. The building is crowned with a glass cantilevered block with telescopic views of the city.

© TCHOBAN VOSS Architekten

architects
SPEECH architectural office,
TCHOBAN VOSS Architekten

type
museum

construction
2012

24. Greifswalder Office Building

Greifswalder Straße 226
10405 Berlin

external viewing only

 142 / 200 >
Am Friedrichshain

 M4 > Am Friedrichshain

This office building is set on a 464 square metre corner plot, completing the city block. Internally it opens onto a private courtyard with a small garden. The six-floor building houses offices, co-working spaces, stores and rental units. The steel frame and tempered glass of the ground floor façade creates a strong effect in contrast with the dark walls that mark the entrance, accentuating the central structure. The first five floors of the building have a powerful design, featuring a square concrete grid system that projects 50 centimetres from the façade. The rigidity of the structural grid is softened by the organic effect of the concrete profile that creates an alternating wave pattern and a play of light and shadow during the day. On the roof of the building, the top floor is recessed one and a half metres from the façade to form a continuous terrace walkway that follows the entire perimeter.

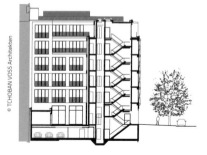

© TCHOBAN VOSS Architekten

architects
TCHOBAN VOSS Architekten

type
offices

construction
2019

25. CB19

Christburger Straße 19
10405 Berlin

external viewing only

CB19 was realised without the support of a construction company, but was managed as a joint venture between the future owners, following the formula of every project by zanderrotharchitekten. The in-house development company SmartHoming developed each project from the search for the land until each owner moved into their flat, managing the *Baugruppe* until the end. This system provided far better control of financing during construction and greater freedom in decisions concerning the interiors and finishes for each family. The internal space is a large open layout thanks to the long single span ceilings, that have eliminated internal bearing walls. The only fixed elements are the elevator shafts; this has provided great freedom for designing the internal layout according to the needs of each resident. The front and back façades differ for their character and choice of materials: the street façade features large, full height, fixed picture windows, vast urban display cases, that amplify the contact between interior and exterior. The rear façades were designed with long continuous concrete terrace balconies that provide direct access to the fire escape stairways.

M4 /M10 >
Greifswalder Straße/
Danziger Straße

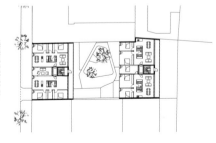

© zanderrotharchitekten

architects
zanderrotharchitekten

type
residential

construction
2015

26. Velodrom and Schwimm-und Sprunghalle im Europasportpark

Paul-Heyse-Straße 26
10407 Berlin

open to the public

+49 (0) 30 42 18 60

S8 / S41 / S42 / S85 >
Landsberger Allee

156 / M8 >
Landsberger Allee

**M4 / M5 / M6 / M8
/ M10** > Landsberger
Allee

The Velodrom and Schwimm-und Sprunghalle im Europasportpark project, designed by Dominique Perrault, was developed for the competition to host the 2000 Olympic Games (won by Sydney). The centre is built on a large 24 acre, rectangular site, set between two districts on the eastern side of the city. The opportunity of creating an urban continuum was exploited with the drawing up of a simple masterplan based on a low-impact structure. The vast rectangular site was divided into two pure geometrical forms: a circle and a rectangle. The roofs are almost on a level with the ground in the public green space. This effect was obtained by excavating the site and building the two structures partially underground. The buildings were clad in metal mesh so they would blend with the landscape and be visible only from a short distance. The roofing is raised on lattice structures, 4 metres high, to conceal the technical equipment and to also create a powerful scenographic effect, since the natural light penetrates the buildings around the entire perimeter.

© Dominique Perrault Architecture

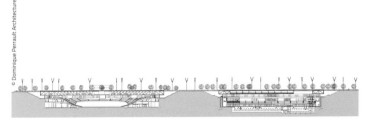

architect
Dominique Perrault
Architecture

type
sports centre

construction
1992-1997

27. Haus Lemke

Oberseestraße 60
13053 Berlin

Tue - Sun / 10 am - 5 pm

+49 (0) 30 97 00 06 18

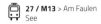
27 / M13 > Am Faulen See

This house, commissioned by the art collector Karl Lemke, was Mies van der Rohe's last project before his exile in the United States, built during the brief period when he was director of the Bauhaus school. It encapsulates all the elements of his research into spatial organisation and different materials. The walls become partitions that plastically model the internal space, creating a fluid movement with a visual connection between the interior and the garden designed by Karl Foerster. The project was based on a L-shaped layout built to enclose an external courtyard. The architectural design is simple, solid and functional, where the outer brick walls are interrupted by the elegant steel and glass design of the large square windows that overlook the Obersee Lake. The interiors were designed by Mies van der Rohe and Lilly Reich; the furnishings and decor in each room were built with woods in a limited palette in perfect coherence with the minimalist design, leaving the space clear to display a few decorative papyrus pieces. This valuable example of Modernist architecture was restored between 2000 and 2002 following the disfigurement and alterations it had suffered over time. The family was forced to leave the house, which was occupied by the Soviet army. Later used as a laundry in the 1960s, it was declared a protected heritage building in 1977.

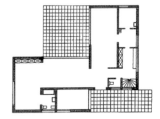

architect
Mies van der Rohe

type
private residence

construction
1932

28. Wohnstadt Carl Legien

Erich-Weinert-Straße
10409 Berlin

external viewing only

 156 > Erich-Weinert-Straße

 M2 > Erich-Weinert-Straße

Wohnstadt Carl Legien (literally: "Carl Legien residential town", named for the German politician and unionist) is a housing estate that is one of the UNESCO World Heritage sites. It was designed in 1925 and built in 1929-30 by Bruno Taut and Franz Hillinger based on the Tussendijken housing estate in Rotterdam, designed by Jacobus Johannes Pieter Oud with whom Taut had numerous contacts. The project is the result of the residential reforms set up during the Weimar Republic in answer to the housing crisis following the First World War. Land in the city centres was becoming far more expensive, forcing architects and constructors to build high density housing, especially in the Prenzlauer Berg quarter. The district was divided into three sites: the first, south of Erich-Weinert-Straße; the second, north of the same street; and the third (never built) further north near Ostseestraße. The composition was based on the *Siedlungen* decree and the façade details are aesthetically and visually different from the nearby Plattenbau housing (typical prefabricated building from the GDR period).

architects
Bruno Taut, Franz Hillinger

type
residential

construction
1925-1930

29. Terrassenhaus Berlin

Böttgerstraße 16
13357 Berlin

external viewing only

 U8 > Berlin-
Gesundbrunnen

 **S1 / S2 / S8 / S25
/ S26 / S42 / S46** >
Berlin-Gesundbrunnen

 247 / N8 / S41 / S42 >
Berlin-Gesundbrunnen

This new mixed-use building is located in a sub-urban area that is mainly composed of early 20th century residential housing. The zone is governed by a 1958 regulatory plan clause that permits only the construction of commercial spaces. However, at the same time, the building must also adhere to the needs of a predominantly residential zone. This contemporary ziggurat answers both requirements, rising vertically to provide a view of the surrounding urban landscape. The concrete structure is composed of staggered, stepped floors that vary in depth, from 26 metres on the ground floor, to 11 metres on the top floor. Each floor opens onto a 6 metre deep terrace that acts as a semi-public communal area. The ground floor opens onto a large covered plaza, over 7 metres deep, connected with the scenographic stairways that run from the public plaza up the entire height of the building.

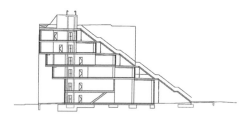

architects
Brandlhuber+ Emde, Burlon,
Muck Petzet Architekten

type
multi-purpose building

construction
2018

30. Park am Nordbahnhof

Gartenstraße 45
13355 Berlin

Mon - Sun / 6 am - 10 pm

This park is located north of the Central Station and was created in a densely built-up area of the city. It was deliberately built along the principal axes of communication, placing the main focus on large wooded areas and uncontrolled grass land to preserve the rural landscape aspect. In contrast with the natural landscape, historic elements have been left as traces and sober reminders for the local population. Large recreational spaces with benches and play areas are located near the ridge of the former railway tracks and the Berlin Wall, indicated with cast iron plaques. The result is a city park, widely used by the population, that creates a division in the inner city fabric, providing green leisure spaces for daily enjoyment.

🚋 **247** > Gartenstrasse/
Feldstraße

architects
FUGMANN JANOTTA
PARTNER

type
public park

construction
2009

31. Kapelle der Versöhnung

Bernauer Straße 4
10115 Berlin

Tue - Sun / 10 am - 5 pm

+49 (0) 30 46 36 034
kirche.versoehnung@berlin.de
www.versoehnungskapelle.de

 U8 > Bernauer Straße

 247 / N8 >
Bernauer Straße

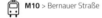 **M10** > Bernauer Straße

This chapel was built on the ruins of the Church of Reconciliation built in 1894, that had survived the two wars until 1961, the year the Berlin Wall was erected. The church was trapped between the eastern and western sections of the Wall and was used as a military observation post until 1985, when it was destroyed. The construction of a new chapel was commissioned by the parish priest as an act of reconciliation between past and future, in contrast with the attitude prevalent at that time which was focused on eliminating every trace of division in Berlin. The Chapel of Reconciliation is a project of rapprochement between the two souls of the city, a place of pacification and remembrance, accentuated by the embracing effect of the slender wooden columns around the external façade that form a corridor of filtered natural light. The internal bearing structure is composed of compressed clay. The chapel contains an original fragment of the altarpiece that survived the destruction of the church.

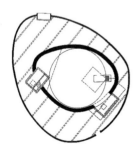

architects
Rudolf Reitermann,
Peter Sassenroth

type
place of worship

construction
2001

32. Museum für Naturkunde (extension)

Invalidenstraße 43
10115 Berlin

Tue - Fri / 9.30 am - 6 pm
Sat - Sun / 10 am - 6 pm

+49 (0) 30 88 91 40 85 91
info@mfn.berlin
www.museumfuernaturkunde.
berlin

N40 >
U Naturkundemuseum

M5 / M8 / M10 >
U Naturkundemuseum

The Museum für Naturkunde was designed by August Tiede and built between 1879 and 1889. In 1917, a fourth wing was added, perpendicular to the original wings, but was destroyed by bombs during the Second World War. The extension and reconstruction involved the destroyed portion of the west wing, and was rebuilt according to the conservation parameters of the original structure. A concrete support shell was constructed using silicone moulds as formwork to cast the concrete façade elements duplicating the bricks and window openings of the existing structure. In the intact portion, the window openings were filled using original bricks, while, in the reconstructed portion, they were closed and recreated in concrete. The blind façades are specifically designed to protect the specimens conserved inside the building. This area contains the collection of 270,000 animal species preserved in formaldehyde, displayed in a striking steel and glass shelving structure, 18 metres high and anchored to the walls.

© Diener & Diener Architekten

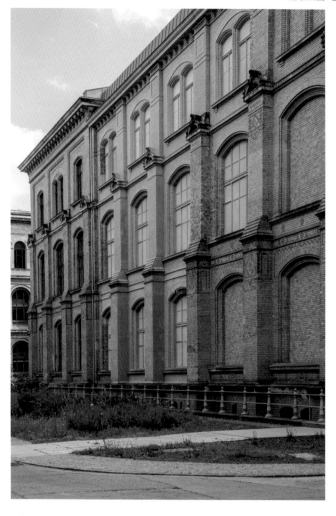

architects
Diener & Diener Architekten

type
museum

construction
2010

33. Slender-Bender

Hessische Straße 5
10115 Berlin

external viewing only

+49 (0) 30 28 59 99 34

 U6 >
U Naturkundemuseum

 N40 >
U Naturkundemuseum
142 / TXL > Robert-
Koch-Platz (Berlin)

**M5 / M6 / M8 /
M10 / 12 >**
U Naturkundemuseum

Slender-Bender is a double project financed by the architects themselves on a very long, narrow urban plot. Bender is the first part of the project: a blend of reconstruction and new-build, it is constructed on a plot 9 metres wide by 14 metres long, with seven floors above ground. The internal layout generates an innovative vertical traffic flow, that is clearly visible in the cross section; there are six mini-lofts, equipped with all home comforts, that can be rented for short to medium term lease, as an alternative to a hotel, or for use as retail stores or office space. Every area is flooded with natural light which penetrates the building through the full height slots in the façade. The two top floors are reserved for Slender, an apartment with a private garden that can cater for a family. Different spaces have been realised thanks to the double height ceilings and angles that create a very dynamic layout. The façades feature three stainless steel ribbons that accentuate the curving profiles, with a play of unexpected reflections that give the entire structure a futuristic look.

© Deadline

architects
Deadline

type
residential

construction
2003

34. Futurium Berlin

Alexanderufer 2
10117 Berlin

Fri - Mon, Wed /
10 am - 6 pm
Thu / 10 am - 8 pm
Tue / closed

+49 (0) 30 40 81 89 777

www.futurium.de

 U55 > Berlin Central
Station

 S3 / S5 / S7 / S9 >
Berlin Hauptbahnhof

 **120 / 123 / 142 / 147
/ 245 / M41 / M85 /
N20 / N40 / RE7 / TXL**
> Berlin Central Station

 M5 / M8 / M10 >
Berlin Central Station

Futurium Berlin is home of an exhibition and conference centre dedicated to questions and discussions about future. The building is positioned crosswise in comparison to the urban grid and is set back from the street line creating a new relationship with its context by interrupting the strict façades of the surrounding institutional buildings. The two entrances on the northern and southern sides are emphasised by cantilevered canopies that extend out for 18 metres to form large covered public spaces. The façades are clad in over 8,000 metal and glass, back-ventilated, rhomboid panels. The 70×70 centimetres panels consist of folded metal reflectors and textured glass with a ceramic print. The internal space is spread over two floors above ground and one below ground. The ground floor houses the foyer, a restaurant, a shop and event spaces. The basement is home to the "Futurium Lab", a double height space, measuring 600 square metres, paved with asphalt stone slabs, and lit by 126 fluorescent screens . The upper floor forms a triple zone exhibition area covered by a "Skywalk" roof terrace clad with solar panels.

© Richter Musikowski

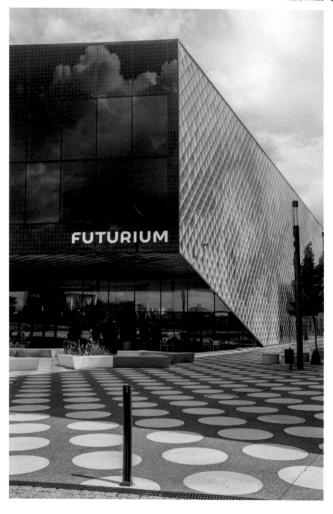

architect
Richter Musikowski

type
museum

construction
2017

35. Marie-Elisabeth-Lüders-Haus and Paul-Löbe-Haus

**Adele-Schreiber-Krieger-
Straße 1**
10117 Berlin

external viewing only

+49 (0) 30 22 70

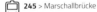

U55 > Bundestag

245 > Marschallbrücke

This structure, better known as the Third Parliament Building, was named after Marie Elisabeth Lüders, a politician and women's rights activist, and the first woman in Germany to obtain a doctorate in 1912. The official reception building overlooks the River Spree and is designed in relation to the nearby Paul-Löbe-Haus, two projects that are part of the "Federal Row" masterplan in a dialogue of large open steel and glass structures surmounted by extremely light roofing supported by slender concrete pillars. This dialogue continues even more strongly from east to west with the creation of a series of public squares – Spreeplatz – that mitigate the rupture, both visual and geographical, of the area where the Wall once stood. Traces of the division still remain even inside the Marie Elisabeth Lüders building, shown in a work by Ben Wagin who reconstructed some concrete panels that indicate the years between the construction and the fall of the Wall, and marking the number of ascertained victims in each year.

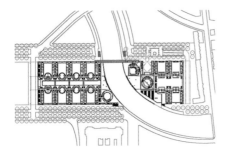

architect
Stephan Braunfels

type
offices

construction
2003

C

Mitte – Tiergarten

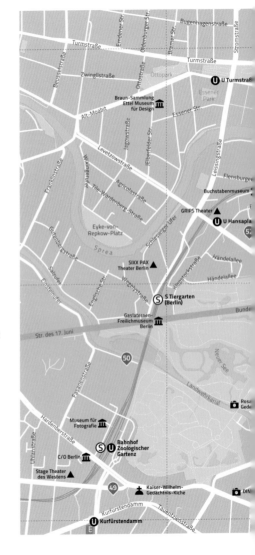

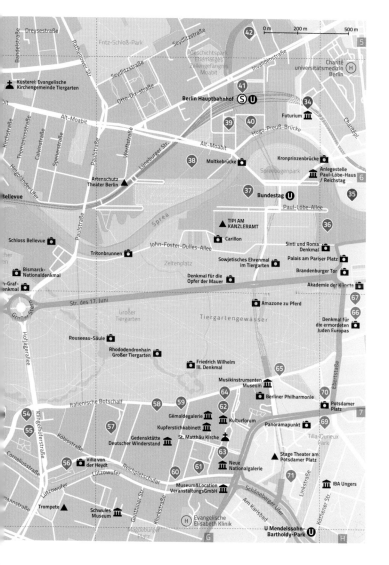

Dreysestraße
Fritz-Schloß-Park
Seydlitzstraße
Bandelstraße
Rathenower Str.
Seydlitzstraße

42

0 m   200 m   500 m

Geschichtspark
Ehemaliges
Zellengefängnis
Moabit

Invalidenstraße

Charité
universitätsmedizin (H)
Berlin

Otto-Dix-straße

Küsterei: Evangelische
Kirchengemeinde Tiergarten

41

Berlin Hauptbahnhof (S)(U)

34

Futurium 🏛

Alt-Moabit

Kirchstraße
Thomasiusstraße
Calvinstraße
Spenerstraße
Paulstraße
Werftstraße
Lüneburger Str.

39   40

Hugo-Preuß-Brücke

Charitépl.

Alt-Moabit

38   Moltkebrücke 📷

Kronprinzenbrücke 📷

Artenschutz
Theater Berlin ▲

Spreebogenpark

Anlegestelle
Paul-Löbe-Haus
/ Reichstag 🏛

Bellevue

37   Bundestag (U)

Paul-Löbe-Allee

35

Paulstraße

Spree

TIPI AM
KANZLERAMT ▲

36

Schloss Bellevue 📷

Carillon 📷

Sinti und Roma
Denkmal 📷

Tritonbrunnen 📷

John-Foster-Dulles-Allee

Palais am Pariser Platz 📷

Zeltenplatz

Sowjetisches Ehrenmal
im Tiergarten 📷

Brandenburger Tor 📷

Bismarck-
Nationaldenkmal 📷

Denkmal für die
Opfer der Mauer 📷

Akademie der Künste 📷

-Graf-
enkmal 📷

Str. des 17. Juni

Amazone zu Pferd 📷

67

66

Großer
Tiergarten

Tiergartengewässer

Denkmal für
die ermordeten
Juden Europas 📷

Rousseau-Säule 📷

Hofjägerallee

Rhododendronhain
Großer Tiergarten 📷

Friedrich Wilhelm
III. Denkmal 📷

Musikinstrumenten
Museum 🏛

65

Berliner Philharmonie 📷

70

Italienische Botschaft

58   59

64

62

Potsdamer
Platz

54

Gemäldegalerie 🏛

Kulturforum

Panoramapunkt 📷

Klingelhöferstraße
Köbisstraße

57

Kupferstichkabinett 🏛

Tilla-Durieux-
Park

55

Gedenkstätte
Deutscher Widerstand 🏛

St. Matthäu Kirche ▲

69

Corneliusstraße

56   Villa von
der Heydt 📷

Reichpietschufer

63   Neue
Nationalgalerie 🏛

Stage Theater am
Potsdamer Platz ▲

Eberstraße

Lützowufer

71

IBA Ungers 🏛

nannstraße

Trompete ▲

Gentinthiner Str.
Klückstraße

60   61

Museum&Location
VeranstaltungsGmbH 🏛

Schöneberger Ufer

Am Karlsbad

Linkstraße

Köthener Str.

Schwules
Museum 🏛

Magdeburger
Platz

(H) Evangelische
Elisabeth Klinik

U Mendelssohn-
Bartholdy-Park (U)

G   H

36. Deutscher Bundestag (Reichstag extension)

Platz der Republik 1
11011 Berlin

Mon - Sun / 8 pm - 12 am

+49 (0) 30 22 73 71 71
pressereferat@bundestag.de
www.bundestag.de

 U55 > Bundestag

 100 > Reichstag/
Bundestag

This extension and reconstruction project was based on four cornerstone principles: the constitution of a democratic forum, the German Parliament, an understanding of the country's history, the commitment to promoting a focus on accessibility and environmental issues. So the project reflects the momentum for reconstruction typical of post-war projects which, especially in this case, needed to represent the new democratic Germany: a country anchored in its past and leaning towards a transparent and innovative future, represented by the great cupola. The core of the project is the dome that acts on an urban scale as a landmark that is recognisable day and night. It is a centripetal element able to introject and catalyse attention through its sculptural light. The dome is a sustainable technical element that provides natural ventilation and light thanks to the distinctive inverted pyramid system that reflects light down into the parliament chamber. The public can visit the interior of the dome using the double helical ramp built around the perimeter of the structure up to a panoramic viewing area and restaurant at the top.

© Drawn by BPR for Foster + Partners

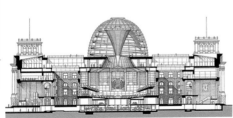

architects
Foster + Partners

type
institutional building

construction
1999

37. Federal Chancellery

Willy-Brandt-Straße 1
10557 Berlin

external viewing only

+49 (0) 30 18 27 22 720

www.bundesregierung.de/
breg-de/bundesregierung/
bundeskanzleramt

 U55 > Bundestag

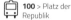 **100** > Platz der
Republik

The German Federal Chancellery (Bundeskanzle-ramt) concludes and continues the façade of government administrative buildings on both banks of the River Spree. It is a concrete structure that follows the boundary wall around the Chancellery gardens, designed by Lützow 7 landscape architects, defining the semi-circular perimeter of the property in a dialogue with the pre-existent building on the opposite bank of the Spree. The vast concrete cube is interrupted by harmonious full-height slots in the façade and very slender partitions that add dynamic movement to the strict rectangular lines. These openings create a transparent communication between the public spaces and the government offices. The façade windows are reflected in the large formal internal spaces faced with granite, where the clean, orderly, minimal lines reflect the solemn, official character of the building.

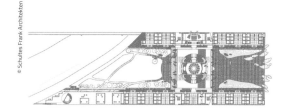

architects
Schultes Frank Architekten

type
institutional building

construction
2001

38. Fire and Police station (extension)

Elisabeth-Abegg-Straße 2
10115 Berlin

external viewing only

 U55 > Berlin Central
Station

 S3 / S5 / S7 / S9 >
Berlin Hauptbahnhof

 **120 / 123 / 142 / 147
/ 245 / M41 / M85
/ N20 / N40 / TXL** >
Berlin Central Station

 M5 / M8 / M10 >
Berlin Central Station

The Fire and Police station extension was built attached to an existing building dating from the 19th century on the banks of the River Spree. The project involved the annexation of a new contemporary extension, a "backbone" designed to unify the various departments, service areas, and police car parking area. The distinctive element of the new projects is the entrance on the second floor, accessible by a transparent footbridge leading directly from the street 6 metres above the ground floor, creating a visual and physical connection with the surrounding landscape. The façades are in stark contrast with the rough brickwork of the existing building. They are clad in glass louvre shingles recalling fish scales, in colours ranging from brick red to forest green and light green. The shingles are 65 centimetres high and between a metre and two and half metres long.

© Sauerbruch Hutton

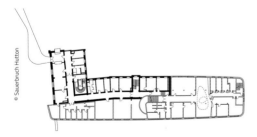

architects
Sauerbruch Hutton

type
police and fire station

construction
2004

39. Bertha Berlin

Bertha-Benz-Straße
10557 Berlin

external viewing only

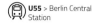
U55 > Berlin Central Station

120 / 123 / 142 / 147 / 245 / M41 / M85 / N20 / N40 / RE7 / TXL > Berlin Central Station

M5 / M8 / M10 > Berlin Central Station

This office block is the fourth and last building that completes the Lehrter Stadtquartier masterplan, designed in 1994 by Oswald Mathias Ungers. The building had to adhere to limits regarding height, volume and construction materials, established during the planning of the other three blocks, to present a flat façade on the main street, while the sides facing the interior have an undulating dynamic surface. The façades feature narrow vertical fins of Sellenberger Muschelkalk – a natural stone used traditionally in local construction. Each section of the double façade varies in height and thickness, helping to lighten the overall impact of the building, with a vibrant effect within the surrounding urban fabric. The double height base of the construction connects with the square in front of the building, creating a continuous flow between exterior and interior. The ground floor houses retail stores, while the upper floors are dedicated to office space. A terrace is located on the ninth floor.

© Barkow Leibinger

architect
Barkow Leibinger

type
offices

construction
2014-2016

40. cube berlin

Washingtonpl. 3
10557 Berlin

external viewing only

M29 / N8 >
U Moritzplatz

The opening of the new main railway station in 2006 marked the starting point for the development of the Washingtonplatz district and the new masterplan for Europacity. cube berlin occupies a unique position in this context as it has free exposure on all sides: it is opposite the Federal Government Complex on the other side of the Spree, it sits alongside the Hauptbahnhof (Central Station), and is in the centre of a vast plaza. The building resembles a huge glazed kaleidoscope that reflects all the surrounding buildings; a dynamic outer glass skin with changing geometries is wrapped around the building to form panoramic viewing terraces and large public entrances. cube berlin is one of the most innovative smart buildings in Europe, setting new standards for the integration of intelligent digital interfacing to enable interaction with visitors, engaging them to be more aware of energy saving behaviour. Sustainability is an integral part of the project design: the thermal insulating façades create constant natural air ventilation: the internal micro-climate and lighting are controlled by a "self-learning brain" that detects all building "behaviour" in order to improve performance.

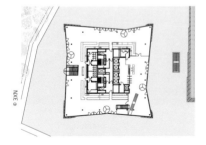

© NXE

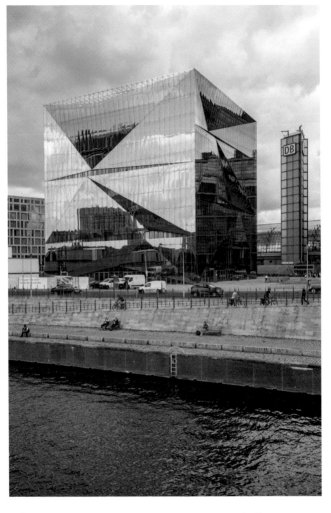

architects
3XN

type
offices

construction
2020

41. Berlin Hauptbahnhof

Europaplatz 1
10557 Berlin

open to the public

+49 (0) 180 6 99 66 33

www.bahnhof.de

 S3 / S5 / S7 / S9 >
Berlin Hauptbahnhof

 **120 / 123 / 142 / 147
/ 245 / M41 / M85 /
N20 / N40 / RE7 / TXL**
> Berlin Hauptbahnhof

 M5 / M6 / M8 / M10 >
Berlin Hauptbahnhof

© gmp · Architects von Gerkan, Marg and Partners

Berlin Hauptbahnhof (Berlin Central Station) is the largest multi-level station in Europe. Inaugurated in 2006, it was actually imagined almost a century before, but never built because of the two wars. The station is located on the site of the Lehrter Bahnhof, which was the last station in West Germany before reaching Friedrichstraße on the former border with East Germany. This is a monumental structure because of the technology that was necessary during the ten years of its construction which included deviating the course of the River Spree. The vast steel and glass structure dominates the whole area, stretching 160 metres from north to south, 320 from east to west, with two office blocks 46 metres high, and 780 solar panels that supply a small percentage of the station's energy requirements. The hub of the station is composed of five different levels, and caters to 300,000 passengers a day. The rail tracks run on the highest and lowest levels, while the other three contain retail stores, restaurants, offices, and supermarkets, that communicate via 54 escalators and elevators, both standard and panoramic. The station is a city within the city, and has become an original tourist attraction, as well as the heart around which new leading edge urban sectors are being developed.

architects
gmp · Architekten von Gerkan, Marg und Partner

type
railway station

construction
2006

42. Tour Total and Monnet 4

Jean-Monnet-Straße 4
10557 Berlin

external viewing only

 U55 > Berlin Central Station

 120 / 142 / 147 / 245 / N20 / N40 / TXL > Invalidenpark

 M5 / M8 / M20 > Invalidenpark

These two buildings, constructed three years apart, both belong to the Europacity masterplan surrounding the main railway station. They were initially planned as a single closed block but were later built as separate structures in dialogue with each other at the same time. The composition similarity is suggested by the empty space around the towers to provide visual and functional connection between the buildings and the neighbourhood. This dialogue is accentuated by the choice of construction materials and the façade surfaces: the Tour Total is faced with exposed precast concrete bearing columns to create a strict squared impact, while the Monnet 4 has a lightweight curtain wall composed of a double layer of aluminium fins partially detached from the internal wall. Both buildings feature double height formal lobbies, with a well grounded aspect thanks to the tapering asymmetrical columns at ground floor level, and the fine shimmering aluminium fins on Monnet 4, designed to control the sun's rays.

© Barkow Leibinger

architect
Barkow Leibinger

type
offices

construction
2010-2015

43. Siedlung Schillerpark

Bristolstraße 1, 2, 5
13349 Berlin

external viewing only

 U6 > Seestraße

 106 / 120 / N6 / N20 / N26 > Seestraße

 50 / M13 > Osram-Höfe

The Siedlung Schillerpark (Schillerpark Settlement) was one of the first metropolitan housing projects built in Berlin during the Weimar Republic period, along with other housing projects suspended during the First World War. It was promoted by the building reforms introduced in 1924 and was based on a revision of low-cost housing, introducing new compositional planning which no longer ruled that buildings had to be constructed along the street front, but could be integrated freely in the surrounding landscape. The exposed brick façades and flat roof, plus the blue and white ceramic profiling, are clearly inspired by the Modernist Movement. The apartments vary in size, from 40 square metres to spacious four-roomed apartments with loggias or balconies. This district was partially rebuilt after Second World War, firstly by Bruno Taut's brother, Max, and between 1954 and 1959, by Hans Hoffmann, who designed the expansion project based on the original plans by Bruno Taut.

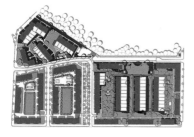

architect
Bruno Taut

type
residential

construction
1924-1930

44. AEG Turbinenhalle

Huttenstraße
10553 Berlin

external viewing only

M27 > Reuchlinstraße

The AEG turbine factory is considered a milestone in the history of 20th century architecture; a masterpiece of German Proto-rationalism applied to industrial buildings. With this structure, Behrens included new archetypes never before associated with industrial construction, transforming work spaces into places of worship dedicated to mechanics and innovation, temples of work and progress: in the words of Sigfried Giedion, "Behrens consciously transformed places of human activity into dignified locations". The open plan turbine factory building is surmounted by a row of 14 tapering steel columns, 9.22 metres apart, that support the imposing gabled framing. The side façades incorporate full height windows to provide natural light inside the factory; alternating concrete sections with rounded corners are deliberately recessed into the façade to underline their non-structural role. The street façade is topped with a polygonal gable that bears the company's logo in large letters.

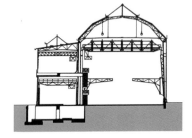

architects
Peter Behrens, Karl Bernhard

type
industrial building

construction
1908-1909

45. Corbusierhaus

Flatowallee 16
14055 Berlin

open to the public
by appointment

www.corbusierhaus-berlin.de

S3 / S9 >
Olympiastadion

218 / M49 >
Flatowallee/
Olympiastadion

This residential block, clearly based on the model of the 'Unité d'Habitation', or 'Housing Unit', was built for the international residential housing exhibition in West Berlin in 1957, the Interbau 57. The changes made to the building during construction under the Interbau 57 direction were so radical that Le Corbusier refused to recognise his design. Originally conceived to resemble his other Unités d'Habitation, the Corbusierhaus was completely deprived of its public functions like the roof terrace, and other common areas were reduced by half to create more apartments. The 18-floor structure is built on a 3,600 square metre site, and houses 557 apartments, 22 more than originally planned. The characteristic pilotis for the ground floor parking were replaced by transversal bearing partitions. Like the interiors of the building, the exposed concrete walls were painted in much less vibrant colours than those of the Unités d'Habitation built in France.

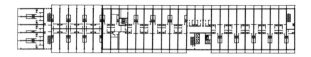

architect
Le Corbusier

type
residential

construction
1958

46. Heinz-Galinski-Schule Charlottenburg

Waldschulallee 73
14055 Berlin

external viewing only

+49 (0) 30 30 11 940
kontact@hsgberlin.de
www.hgsberlin.de

S3 / S9 > S Messe Süd

349 > S Messe Süd

The project for the Heinz-Galinski School is unusual for its golden spiral layout, as well as for the references to Jewish traditions and culture since this was the first Jewish school built after the Holocaust. The architect's idea was to create a series of sections able to capture natural daylight throughout the day. With its complex organic layout the school has adapted to and lives within its community, like a children's citadel that changes during the day: the central patio becomes a playground during recreation times, while the intricate maze of alleys and corridors spread out leading to the classrooms. The complex is based on Deconstructivism, and is composed of large wedge-shaped sections that rotate around the internal courtyard. These sections house the classrooms and office spaces.

© Zvi Hecker Architect

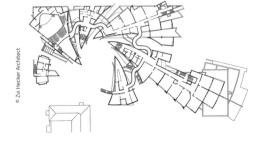

architect
Zvi Hecker Architect

type
education

construction
1993

47. Internationale Congress Centrum ICC

Messedamm 22
14057 Berlin

external viewing only

+49 (0) 30 30 380
central@messe-berlin.de
www.messe-berlin.de

 S3 / S9 > S Messe Süd

 349 > Messegelände/
Verwaltung

The ICC is one of the most important congress centres in Europe. Built in 1979, it is a magnificent example of Postmodern architecture, running 320 metres along the city motorway to emphasise its direct contact with technology and progress. Its colossal, rather forbidding aspect has led to its being described as Sci-Fi and Futuristic in design because of the metal sheet cladding on the complex profiles. The central building is embraced by enormous structural beams to underline its functional nature, like the distribution towers that support the structural elements. The only openings toward the exterior are the ribbon windows with rounded corners that soften the Modernistic appearance of the centre.

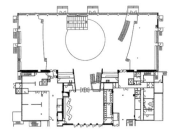

architects
Ralf Schüler,
Ursulina Schüler-Witte

type
congress centre

construction
1979

48. Aesop

Fasanenstraße 74
10719 Berlin

Mon - Sat / 11 am - 7 pm

+49 (0) 30 88 72 88 28
fasanenstrasse@aesop.com
www.aesop.com

 U1 > U Uhlandstraße

 109 / 110 / M19 / M29 / N10 / X10 > U Uhlandstraße

This 93 square metre store drew its inspiration from the historic context of the neighbourhood, home to dozens of small cultural centres and performing arts theatres. The interior is furnished with mobile oak panel columns that open up to form cabinets for product display, in perfect harmony with the same oak flooring; the cabinets and floor are highlighted by the contrasting dark-coloured walls. By day the cabinets are open to display the store's products, while at night their side doors close to form thick oak columns that visually surround the large central counter. The product display cabinets are structural elements designed with a dual function, using innovative joinery and carpentry techniques and sliding systems set into floor guide tracks. The clever downlighting gives the store a dramatic theatrical atmosphere, in a clear allusion to the neighbouring Theatre des Westens and the Berliner Schaubühne.

architects
Snøhetta

type
retail

construction
2014

49. Upper West

Kantstraße 165
10623 Berlin

open to the public

+49 (0) 30 32 29 31 900
berlin-upperwest@motel-
one.com
www.motel-one.com/en/
hotels/berlin/hotel-berlin-
upper-west/

 U1 / U9 >
Kurfürstendamm

 **109 / 110 / 204 / 249
/ M19 / M29 / M46
/ N1 / N2 / N3 / N9
/ N10 / N26 / X10** >
Kurfürstendamm

Upper West is a majestic skyscraper, 118 metres tall, that stands out against the skyline, towering over the nearby Kaiser Wilhelm Memorial Church and Berlin Zoo Station. The high-rise complex has a total area of 53,000 square metres and houses office spaces, retail stores and luxury apartments. The central portion is occupied by an exclusive hotel, topped by a lounge bar with panoramic views of the city. The architecture is a monolithic structure composed of an eight-storey foundation base for the sinuous tower with its curved rounded corners. The building is clad with a concrete skin that forms a very malleable mesh of polygonal elements that clad the slightly curved grid surface, with its 3,700 windows, 694 specifically designed profiles, and the 93 elements for the terraces. The initial Upper West building, then called Atlas Tower, was designed in 1994, but the construction was delayed for over twenty years because of changes in government and the 2008 economic crisis. Another reason was the petition to boycott the demolition of the Schimmelpfeng-Haus that was located in the area, an architectural monument that was considered an integral part of Berlin's historical-cultural heritage.

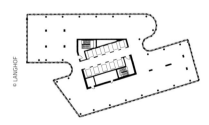

© LANGHOF

architects
LANGHOF

type
hotel

construction
2017

50. UT 2 – Umlauftank 2

Müller-Breslau-Straße 12
10623 Berlin

external viewing only

U2 / U3 / U9 >
Stazione di Berlin
Zoologischer Garten

**100 / 109 / 110 / 200
/ 204 / 245 / 249 /
M45 / M46 / M49 /
N1 / N2 / N9 / N10 /
N26 / X9 / X10 / X34 >**
Hertzallee

Umlauftank 2 (circulation tank), known as the "pink tube", is the headquarters of the Research Institute for Hydraulic Engineering and Ship-building of the Technical University of Berlin, founded in 1903 by Wilhelm II. The building is located on the Landwehr Canal on the western tip of the Tiergarten, and was named a herit-age site in 1995. The extension by Ludwig Leo in 1973 was built on top of a horizontal brick building overlooking the river, with tall arched windows dating from the 1950s. Leo's proposal was in complete contrast with the pre-existing building, with all the focus on the equipment and technical structures: the main feature is the pink tube, 7 metres in diameter, that crosses the floating metal cube structure. An urban pop sculpture that does not conceal its true function but underlines its expressive potential. In 2012 a restoration campaign was launched to restore the equipment for safety reasons, removing the asbestos and maintaining the structure as close to the original design as possible.

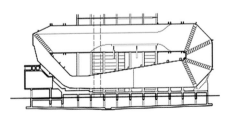

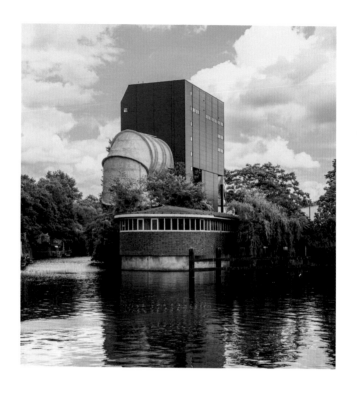

architect
Ludwig Leo

type
research institute

construction
1973

51. PTB – Physikalisch-Technische Bundesanstalt

Abbestraße 2
10587 Berlin

external viewing only

+49 (0) 30 34 810
info@ptb.de
www.ptb.de

 U2 > U-Bhf Ernst-Reuter-Platz

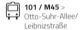 **101 / M45** >
Otto-Suhr-Allee/
Leibnizstraße

This project is part of the Physical Park of the PTB Institute. It is composed of an insertion into the landscape that has been developed and expanded underground; thanks to the gently folded roof, it creates a visual link and dialogue with the existing buildings. Below the highest section of the green roof is the main entrance and a wide staircase leading down to the hall where the traffic flow is directed between the new extension and the existing complex, directly connected to the underground structure. The laboratories, waiting rooms, and service areas, with changing rooms and lockers, all have natural lighting. This is achieved through the layout arranged around a central light shaft. The façades above ground are composed of large glass windows and columns are clad with polished stainless steel panels, to reflect the surrounding park.

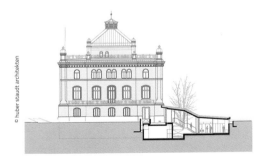

© huber staudt architekten

architects
huber staudt architekten

type
research institute, offices

construction
2012

52. Interbau Apartment House

Altonaer Straße 6
10557 Berlin

external viewing only

 U9 > U Hansaplatz

 S3 / S5 / S7 / S9 > Bellevue

 106 / N26 > U Hansaplatz

Together with Le Corbusier, Oscar Niemeyer was also invited to participate in the international residential housing exhibition, Interbau 57, with avant-garde Modernist solutions. The Brazilian architect's project is an example of clean lines and Modernist precision, and has been preserved in perfect condition to the present day. The residential apartment building is composed of a long narrow concrete slab, supported on refined V-shaped pillars, slightly rotated and recessed from the façade line. The building seems lightly suspended above the ground although it is supported by cubes clad with small red and blue mosaic tiles that conceal the stairways. The façade features uniform windows and loggias decorated with mosaics in primary colours. Next to the building is the elevator tower accessed by walkways on the fifth and seventh floors. This vertical element recalls the services tower that Lina Bo Bardi created at the SESC Pompeia in 1977.

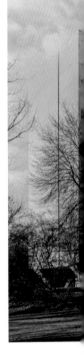

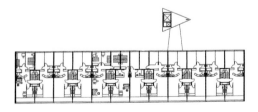

architects
Oscar Niemeyer,
Soares Filho

type
residential

construction
1957

53. Stadtvilla Rauchstraße

Rauchstraße 4-10
10785 Berlin

external viewing only

 200 > Corneliusbrücke

Stadtvilla Rauchstraße was part of a housing scheme operation by Land Berlin that commissioned Rob Krier to supervise the masterplan and the drawing up of the guidelines for the individual buildings. The project was composed of nine residential buildings designed by famous architects including Aldo Rossi, Giorgio Grassi, Brenner & Tonon and Hans Hollein. The purpose was to balance the privacy requirements of the residents, setting houses further back from the street and providing closer contact with nature. The buildings were set on raised ground that sloped down to street level and were distanced from one another around a rectangular common garden. The Haus 8 building was designed by Hans Hollein: the square layout was interrupted by two crossed directrix lines that break up the rigidity of the plan. The result can be seen on the façade with the concave and convex floors that add movement to the severe cubic design required in the guidelines, obtained thanks to the pastel blue and pink shades. The design by Grassi (Haus 3) presents four inward facing tower elements, painted white with contrasting metal window frames. Haus 4 by Valentiny and Hermann features blue façades, interrupted by a cream and orange striped base and orange roof trim.

architects
Rob Krier (urban planning),
Valentiny/Hermann, Brenner/
Tonon, Nielbock&Partners,
Aldo Rossi, Giorgio Grassi,
Hans Hollein

type
residential

construction
1984

54. Nordic Embassies (masterplan)

Rauchstraße 1
10785 Berlin

Mon - Fri / 10 am - 7 pm
Sat - Sun / 11 am - 4 pm

+49 (0) 30 50 500
info@nordischebotschaften.
org
www.nordischebotschaften.
org

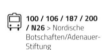
**100 / 106 / 187 / 200
/ N26** > Nordische
Botschaften/Adenauer-
Stiftung

This project unites the embassies of five Nordic countries in the same complex (Denmark, Finland, Iceland, Norway and Sweden) to physically demonstrate their cohesion and similar geopolitical views and actions. The composition is based on the subtraction of portions of the principal structure and the morphological line of the surrounding main urban roads. The result is an organic structure divided into five elements, each one home to a separate embassy, but physically and visually connected by corridors and internal plazas that act as communal spaces and for public traffic. The five portions are unified by an independent curving wall suspended from the five buildings that runs along the perimeter of the site. It is composed of a band of 3,850 green copper louvres mounted on a steel frame 226 metres long. The louvres can be angled to control light and wind. The central plaza is paved with materials from Sweden and Finland, while all the internal flooring and common spaces are clad in wood to provide a welcoming atmosphere in contrast with the geometrical effect of the exteriors.

© Berger+Parkkinen Architekten

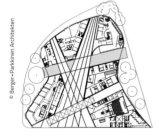

architects
Berger+Parkkinen
Architekten

type
institutional building

construction
1999

55. Embassy of Mexico

Klingelhöferstraße 3
10785 Berlin

external viewing only

+49 (0) 30 26 93 230
mexale@sre.gob.mx
https://embamex.sre.gob.mx/
alemania/index.php/es/

**100 / 106 / 187 / 200
/ N26** > Nordische
Botschaften/Adenauer-
Stiftung

The Mexican embassy in Berlin was designed
by architects, Teodoro González de León and
Francisco Serrano, winners of a competition
held in 1977 for an architectural design that
would embody the official representative and
institutional role of the embassy, and at the
same time express the character of a relatively young country, but with an ancient culture. The building features a portico, 18 metres
high, faced with slightly inclined reinforced concrete pillars, interrupted by imposing slots in
the façade that reveal glimpses of the interior.
The massive exterior is in strong contrast with
the atrium roofed by a glass panelled cylinder
18 metres tall and 14 metres deep that creates a light-filled airy entrance foyer. The six-
storey building houses the consular offices, an
internal garden, multi-purpose spaces and the
headquarters of the Mexican Cultural Institute.

architects
Teodoro González de Léon,
Francisco Serrano

type
institutional building

construction
2000

56. Bauhaus-Archiv/Museum für Gestaltung

Knesebeckstraße 1-2
10623 Berlin

temporarily closed
for expansion

www.bauhaus.de

 U2 > U-Bhf Ernst-
Reuter-Platz

 245 / M45 / N2 / X9
> U-Bhf Ernst-Reuter-
Platz

The history of the Bauhaus school archive began much earlier than its design. It was founded by Gropius in Darmstadt to gather the results of the School's laboratory tests and projects, an archive that, in time, grew so large that a specific archive space was needed. Not many documents remain of the original 1964 project because, due to centralised political pressure, the archives were transferred from Darmstadt to Berlin, to a very different site with a natural slope. The remaining elements of that project are the unusual banded profiles and the H-shaped layout composed of a pair of two-floored buildings connected by a central portion that disappears into the landscape. The necessary changes to the initial sketches were made by Alex Cvijanović and the Berlin designer, Hans Bandel. They incorporated the curving entry ramp that interrupts the solid rhythm of the functional façade design. The northern building houses the administration offices, while the southern structures contain 800 and 400 square metre spaces dedicated to permanent and temporary exhibitions. These spaces are flooded with natural daylight that enters through the glazed shed roofing with its slightly rounded profile.

architects
Walter Gropius, Alex
Cvijanović, Hans Bandel

type
museum

construction
1960-1979

57. Landesvertretung Nordrhein-Westfalen

Hiroshimastraße 12-16
10785 Berlin

Mon - Sun / 9 am - 8 pm

+49 (0) 30 27 57 50

This project is located in the heart of the administrative and diplomatic district, and houses the official state representation headquarters of North Rhine-Westphalia. The building was designed as a formal expression of a new type of sustainability, able to perform traditional representational functions combined with a view towards the future. The main structure was designed to express these concepts, encasing and supporting the glass surfaces. The innovative, highly engineered, combination of a steel framework and a wooden parabolic construction coveys a technological atmosphere combined with an urban character, thanks to the internal plaza that connects with the external public space. This public service building manifests architectural design that is the epitome of transparency and aerial lightness.

 M29 > Köbisstraße

© pinkarchitektur

architects	type	construction
pinkarchitektur	offices	2002

58. Embassy of India

Tiergartenstraße 17
10785 Berlin

external viewing only

+49 (0) 30 25 79 53 03

www.indianembassyberlin.
gov.in

The embassy project was the result of an international competition in 1998 won by Léon Wohlhage Wernik Architekten which was commissioned to interpret the intrinsic character of the nation. The main concept was based on Indian craftsmanship and the natural landscape of the country. The most striking aspect is the strong, forceful appearance of the façade. The building is a massive block faced in red Indian stone, rough textured and regular on the façades, revealing circular recessed voids that transmit light into the interior, and give a more technological look. Like traditional Indian buildings, this large reddish cube conceals lush green internal courtyards, overlooked by the offices and official reception rooms.

 200 > Tiergartenstraße

© léonwohlhage

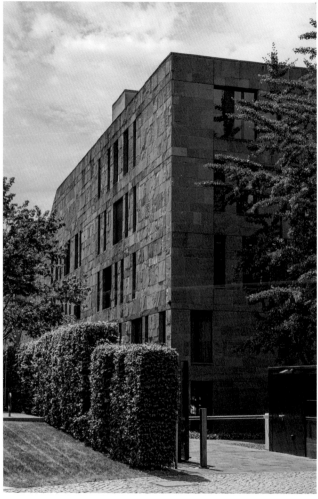

architects
Léon Wohlhage Wernik
Architekten

type
institutional building

construction
2001

59. Embassy of Austria

Stauffenbergstraße 1
10785 Berlin

Mon - Tue, Thu - Fri /
9 am - 1 pm
Wed / 12 am - 4 pm

+49 (0) 30 20 28 70

www.bmeia.gv.at/oeb-berlin

 200 > Tiergartenstraße

The Austrian embassy was designed by Austrian architect and Pritzker Prize winner, Hans Hollein. It is a fine example of Postmodern architecture, charged with citations, references and layering. The building is composed of three elements that distinguish the different functions they perform. The first structure, or consular department, faces east onto Stauffenbergstraße; it recalls the Neoclassical residential buildings typical of the neighbourhood, emphasised by the projecting shelter over the main public entrance. A strict stone parallelepiped is attached to a gentle elliptic element completely clad in copper. This houses the offices spaces and official embassy reception rooms. The consul's office is preceded by a formal double height elliptical entrance, that develops to become a mezzanine floor with an art gallery and a large panoramic window overlooking the Tiergarten. The official area leads directly to the Consul's private residence, in turn connected to the office spaces by a circular glass loggia three storeys tall.

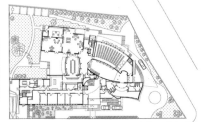

© Private Archive Hollein

architect
Hans Hollein

type
institutional building

construction
2001

60. Shell-Haus

Reichpietschufer 60-62
10785 Berlin

external viewing only

+49 (0) 800 58 93 41 54 46

The Shell-Haus service industry building represents an important example of Modernist architecture, termed Neues Bauen, and was built in 1932 during the Weimar Republic. The complex had to adhere to rigid functional criteria and follow new aesthetic concepts. It was one of the first steel-framed buildings, with an unusual serrated profile on the west side. It is clad in travertine stone from Tivoli and features long bands of rounded ribbon windows. The undulating façade provides a refined flow to this rational and well-balanced structure, enhanced by the sophisticated details like the dark roller shutters in sharp contrast to the light coloured, curved façade.

 M29 > Gedenkstätte
Dt. Widerstand

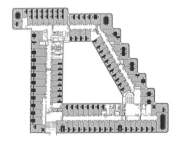

architects
Emil Fahrenkamp

type
offices

construction
1930-1931

61. WZB – Berlin Social Science Center

Reichpietschufer 50
10785 Berlin

Mon - Fri / 9 am - 6.30 pm
Sat - Sun / closed

+49 (0) 30 254910
wzb@wzb.eu
www.wzb.eu

**M29 / M48 / M85 /
N1 / N2** > Potsdamer
Brücke

The office building project designed by Stirling and Wilford was based on the idea of a more informal aspect, more like a university campus than an office block. The complex is composed of various buildings grouped around the former Imperial Insurance Office built by August Busse in 1884.The buildings are arranged in a circle to create a natural urban space, a public open plaza crossed by avenues linked to other parts of the neighbourhood. The multiple architectural references combine and blend with one another: a hexagonal campanile, a long building with porticos and colonnades, a fortified castle and a Greek Stoa enclose the garden. The façades help to create a uniform continuum with alternating bands of terracotta and sky blue; projecting elements in red sandstone frame the windows and create a regular shadow pattern.

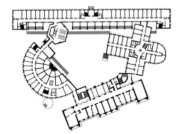

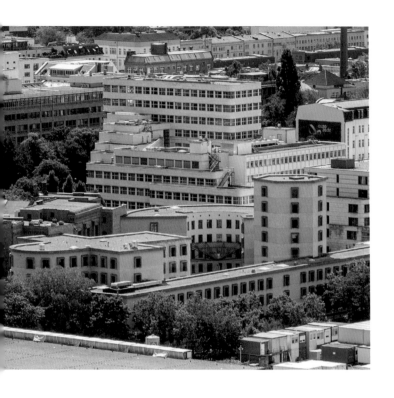

architects
James Stirling, Michael
Wilford & Associates

type
research institute

construction
1987

62. Kulturforum

Matthäikirchplatz 7
10785 Berlin

Tue - Wed, Fri / 10 am - 6 pm
Thu / 10 am - 8 pm
Sat - Sun / 11 am - 6 pm

+49 (0) 30 266 424 242
philipp.eder@kulturforum-
berlin.info
www.kulturforum-berlin.de

M48 / M85 / N2 >
Kulturforum

Similar to the Museum Island in East Berlin, the Kulturforum is a cultural complex set up in the early 1950s in West Berlin, mainly designed by Hans Scharoun, in charge of urban and architectural planning at the time. This area of the city is scattered with buildings that are architecturally diverse, but united in a single masterplan composed of the main museums that house 20th century art. The Kulturforum complex includes the Neue Nationalgalerie (New National Gallery), the Gemaldegalerie (Painting Gallery), the Kupferstichkabinett (Engraving Print Gallery), the Kunstgewerbemuseum (Museum of Decorative Arts), the Philharmonie (Philharmonic Concert Hall), and the Staatsbibliothek (State Library). Two buildings of particular interest are the Painting Gallery and the Philharmonic Concert Hall (Descriptions of the National Gallery and the Decorative Arts Museum are included in this book).

The first building opens like a theatre curtain onto the large public square, creating a threshold for the exhibition space that covers almost 7,000 square metres. The Philharmonic Concert Hall, one of Scharoun's best works, is a masterpiece of engineering with a design that goes beyond the modern. The irregular diamond-shaped layout is carefully modelled according to acoustic research: the parapet details of the balconies, the shape of the seating, the concave and convex roofing all combine to increase the sound quality. The façades clad in yellow perforated metal sheeting also create a link with the nearby Tiergarten.

architects
Hans Scharoun (competition)
/ Hilmer Sattler Architekten
Ahlers Albrecht

type
museum

construction
1964 / 1997

63. Neue Nationalgalerie

Potsdamer Straße 50
10785 Berlin

Tue - Wed, Fri - Sun /
10 am - 6 pm
Thu / 10 am - 8 pm
Mon / closed

+49 (0) 30 266 424 242
service@smb.museum
www.smb.museum

 U1 / U3 / U7 >
U Möckernbrücke

 S1 / S2 / S25 / S26 >
Berlin Potsdamer Platz
Bahnhof

 **M29 / M48 / M85 /
N1 / N2** > Potsdamer
Brücke

The Neue Nationalgalerie is an icon of modern architecture, and was the first building to be completed within the Kulturforum complex. The museum is a light-filled, glazed rectangular pavilion supported by steel pillars, set on a 11×105 metre base that raises the structure above the pedestrian level in front of the building. A temple of modern culture, the museum is built on two levels: the ground floor houses temporary exhibitions, while the basement is home to the permanent collection of avant-garde paintings. The main feature of the design is the support system that provides a single, transparent, completely open space. Eight slender, tapering, cruciform pillars support the roof, 65 metres square and 2 metres high, composed of metal plate sheets on a double T steel beam grid structure. Despite the heavy weight (1,250 tons) the roof structure appears light and seems to be suspended above the exhibition area, deliberately left as an open space for unrestricted viewing. The only interruptions are the marble clad walls that conceal technical equipment, and the mobile partitions that separate the bookshop, office spaces and the café.

architect
Mies van der Rohe

type
museum

construction
1968

64. Kunstgewerbemuseum

Matthäikirchplatz
10785 Berlin

Tue - Wed / 10 am - 6 pm
Sat - Sun / 11 am - 6 pm

+49 (0) 30 266 424 242
service@smb.museum
www.smb.museum

 M48 / M85 / N2 >
Kulturforum

The Kunstgewerbemuseum is the oldest Museum of Decorative and Applied Arts, Design and Fashion in the city. It was founded in 1867, but changed location several times over the decades until it reached its present location, the Kulturforum, considered the core for cultural institutions in Berlin. The building was constructed in 1985 to the design by Rolf Gutbrod, one of the major architects of the 1960s. His architecture is renowned for the visible structural elements on the façades and the creation of communicating internal floors. Between 2012 and 2014, the architectural firm Kuehn Malvezzi was commissioned with the redesign of the fashion, design and Art Nouveau departments as well as the museum's foyer. Their solution relies on the interplay between inside and outside, a clearly structured service area in the entrance foyer, an open course through the redesigned collection departments organized by spaces within spaces, the deliberate staging of exhibits, as well as an easy-to-grasp guidance and information system.

© Kuehn Malvezzi

architects
Rolf Gutbrod /
Kuehn Malvezzi

type
museum

construction
1985 / 2014

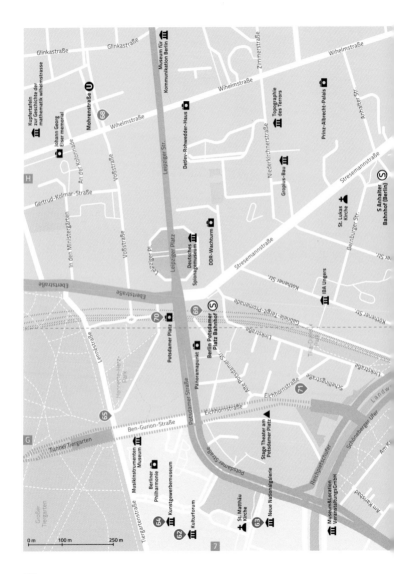

Glinkastraße
Glinkastraße

Kupfertafeln zur Geschichte der mathematik wihelmstrasse

🏛 Museum für Kommunikation Berlin

Zimmerstraße

Wihelmstraße

Wilhelmstraße

🏛 Johann Georg Elser memorial

Mohrenstraße ⓤ

58

Wihelmstraße

🏛 Detlev-Rohwedder-Haus

Leipziger Str.

Niederkirchnerstraße

Anhalter Str.

🏛 Topographie des Terrors

🏛 Prinz-Albrecht-Palais

H

Gertrud-Kolmar-Straße

Voßstraße

In den Ministergärten

Gropius-Bau 🏛

Stresemannstraße

Bernburger Str.

S Anhalter Bahnhof (Berlin) ⓢ

Leipziger Platz

🏛 Deutsches Spionagemuseum

St. Lukas Kirche ✝

DDR-Wachturm

Ebertstraße

Stresemannstraße

Kothener Str.

Ebertstraße

🏛 IBA Ungers

Berlin Potsdamer Platz Bahnhof ⓢ

Gabriele-Tergit-Promenade

69

Panoramapunkt

70

Potsdamer Platz

Linkstraße

Til-D-Park

Kothener Str.

Lennéstraße

Henriette-Herz-Park

Alte Potsdamer Str.

65

Potsdamer Straße

Eichhornstraße

71

Scheidtstraße

Linkstraße

Ben-Gurion-Straße

Eichhornstraße

Schöneberger Ufer

G

Tunnel Tiergarten

Reichpietschufer

Am Karlsbad

Tiergartenstraße

Musikinstrumenten Museum 🏛

Berliner Philharmonie

Kunstgewerbemuseum

Potsdamer Straße

Stage Theater am Potsdamer Platz ▲

Museum&Location VeranstaltungsGmbH 🏛

Großer Tiergarten

64 🏛

62 🏛

Kulturforum

St. Matthäu Kirche ✝

63 🏛 Neue Nationalgalerie

0 m   100 m   250 m

7

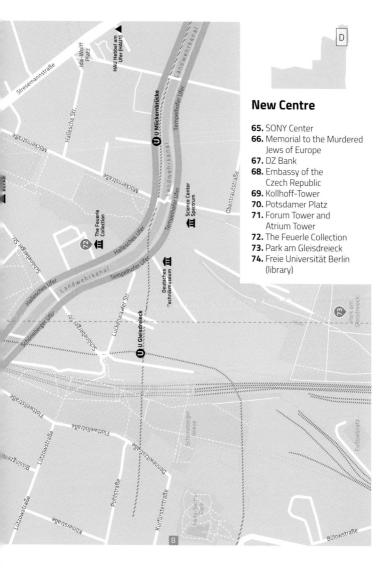

New Centre

65. SONY Center

Potsdamer Straße 4, Kemperplatz
10785 Berlin

Mon - Sat / 11 am - 7 pm

+49 (0) 30 419 555 000

 U2 > U Potsdamer Platz

 S1 / S2 / S25 / S26 / RB10 / RE2 / RE3 / RE4 / RE5 > Berlin Potsdamer Platz Bahnhof

 200 / 300 / M41 / M48 / M85 / N2 > Varian-Fry-Straße/ Potsdamer Platz

The SONY Center is a high tech complex composed of seven buildings covering a surface of 26,000 square metres. It is home to the Japanese Sony headquarters, residential apartments, leisure spaces and offices. It is composed of buildings connected by covered public spaces, with its distinctive glass roof designed by Jahn and Ove Arup & Partners, as a homage to one of Japan's most beloved symbols, Mount Fuji. The oval plaza is covered by a steel and glass umbrella tensile structure skylight attached with tie rods to an enormous steel ring set on the tops of the surrounding buildings. It is dominated by a 3D screen, 25 metres high. The plaza often hosts concerts, film showings, and public events. The roof protects the plaza from the weather, and changes colour according to the time of day and the weather, or using a special electric lighting system. It is about 100 metres long on the longer side and 80 metres long on the shorter side, and covers and area of 4,000 square metres.

architect
Helmut Jahn

type
multi-purpose building,
public space, offices

construction
2000

66. Memorial to the Murdered Jews of Europe

Cora-Berliner-Straße 1
10117 Berlin

Tue - Sat / 10 am - 7 pm

+49 (0) 30 26 39 430

www.stiftung-denkmal.de

 U55 / U2 >
Brandenburger Tor
U Mohrenstr.

 S1 / S2 / S25 / S26 >
Brandenburger Tor

 100 / 245 >
Brandenburger Tor

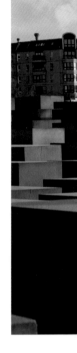

The history of the Holocaust Memorial dates back to 1994, the year the first competition was launched, but without success, until 1997 when a second competition was held, inviting world-famous architects and artists to compete. Despite the winning entry by Eisenman, the official announcement was not made until 1999 and work began only in 2003. The site of the project is the area where the home of Goebbels previously stood, a surface covering 19,000 square metres. It is covered by 2,711 concrete stelae, painted dark grey, each one 2.375 metres long and 95 centimetres wide, in various heights ranging from 20 centimetres to 4 metres. The Memorial was designed to be visited on foot; the symmetry of the orthogonal grid arrangement is broken by the irregular ground surface that dips into a hollow towards the centre. The atmosphere of solitude, anxiety and alienation was created deliberately to show the contrast between an ordered, rational system and the loss of reference and contact with human reason. Below the Memorial is an underground document centre, with information on all the Jews killed in the Shoah, with descriptions of the persecutions, through personal testimonies, images, and letters from the victims.

architects
Eisenman Architects

type
monument

construction
2005

67. DZ Bank

Pariser Platz 3
10117 Berlin

Mon - Fri / 9 am - 6 pm

+49 (0) 30 202 410

www.dzbank.de

U55 >
Brandenburger Tor

S1 / S2 / S25 / S26 >
Brandenburger Tor

100 / 245 >
Brandenburger Tor

Winner of the international bid for tender in 1995, for the DZ Bank headquarters, Gehry designed a building that now houses the bank, a casino, and 39 apartments. The building has two façades: the side housing offices and official meeting rooms is on Pariser Platz in front of the Brandenburg Gate, while the residential side overlooks Behrenstraße. The outer shell respects the strict urban planning regulations leaving the true nature of the building concealed within the interior. The inner façades are composed of large windows in a grid of Vicenza stone similar to the Brandenburg Gate. On the other hand, the residential façade is undulated with stainless steel bow windows. The central atrium connects and divides the traffic flow in various directions towards the casino, the two residential areas and the office space. The Atrium Skylight was developed in close cooperation between the architect and schlaich bergermann partner. It featured a large steel and glass sculpture called "The Whale" and overhead is the remarkable 1,120 square metre skylight, an impressive demonstration of the architect's talent for deconstructive design.

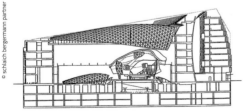

© schlaich bergermann partner

architects
Gehry Partners,
schlaich bergermann partner

type
multi-purpose building,
offices

construction
1998-2000

68. Embassy of the Czech Republic

Wilhelmstraße 44
10117 Berlin

Mon - Fri / 8.30 am - 11 am

+49 (0) 30 226 380
berlin@embassy.mzv.cz
www.mzv.cz/berlin

 U2 > U Mohrenstr.

 300 / M48 / M85 >
U Mohrenstraße

The Embassy of the Czech Republic, built between 1974 and 1979 is located between the Reichsbahndirektion and part of the former Kaiserhof Hotel. A bunker used by Goebbels during the Battle of Berlin in 1943 was discovered during the construction work and later demolished. The massive Brutalist building is a concrete cube measuring 48 metres square, with convex façades on the upper floors that seem to float above the recessed void of the ground floor. The double height staggered first floor has dark reflecting glass, like the ribbon windows around the perimeter of the building. Together with the natural grey stone cladding, these elements give the building an even more solid appearance. In contrast, the interior is decorated in typical 1970s style in warm bright colours: walls are clad in wooden panelling with detailing that changes colour with each room in orange, yellow, blue and green.

architects
Klaus Pätzmann, Vladimir
Machonin, Věra Machoninová

type
institutional building

construction
1972

69. Kollhoff-Tower

Potsdamer Platz 1
10785 Berlin

Mon - Sun / 10 am - 6 pm

 U2 > U Potsdamer Platz

 S1 / S2 / S25 / S26 / RB10 / RE2 / RE3 / RE4 / RE5 > Berlin Potsdamer Platz Bahnhof

 200 / 300 / M41 / M48 / M85 / N2 > Varian-Fry-Straße/ Potsdamer Platz

Among the most famous buildings surrounding Potsdamer Platz, Kollhoff-Tower is one of the most renowned for its design, inspired by early 20th century New York skyscrapers. This reinterpretation of the traditional American model is clearly visible in the brick façade and the base, clad in grey granite, similar to the pavement colour, to mark the atrium open to the public. Like the SONY Center, this tower is an authentic entrance gate between Leipziger Platz and the Kulturforum, in what was formerly the area of division between East and West. The triangular wedge of the 25-storey tower sits on the edge of the plaza; its entrance atrium is in contrast with the irregular structure of the different tower heights designed to integrate with the adjacent buildings. The strict composition of the window distribution is compensated by the dynamic solid brick structure, crowned with gilded keystones.

© Kollhoff Architekten

architects
Hans Kollhoff,
Helga Timmermann

type
offices

construction
2000

70. Potsdamer Platz

Potsdamer Platz 1
10785 Berlin

open to the public

 U2 > U Potsdamer
Platz

 **S1 / S2 / S25 / S26
/ RB10 / RE2 / RE3
/ RE4 / RE5** > Berlin
Potsdamer Platz
Bahnhof

 M29 / N2 >
U Mendelssohn-
Bartholdy-Park

The project to redevelop Potsdamer Platz was part of the masterplan competition won by Renzo Piano Building Workshop in 1992, immediately after the fall of the Wall. The new centre includes two elements that are typical of Berlin: water and green areas, designed to create a new narrative in this area badly destroyed by the Second World War bombing. When the block was completed, the restoration project provided a platform on a human scale, a series of compact seven-storey brick-clad buildings with large windows overlooking public spaces that connected indoor and outdoor areas. On a site with a surface of 68,000 square metres, the buildings provide 350,000 square metres of useable space that house offices, cinemas, apartments, a casino, theatres, restaurants and retail stores. Potsdamer Platz was an opportunity to experiment new construction methods and technological solutions, from the terracotta cladding on façades, to the foundations that demanded marine engineering for the terrain partially affected by water basins.

© Renzo Piano Building Workshop

architects
Renzo Piano Building
Workshop

type
public space

construction
1995

71. Forum Tower and Atrium Tower

Eichhornstraße 3
10785 Berlin

external viewing only

 U2 > U Mendelssohn-Bartholdy-Park

 S1 / S2 / S25 / S26 / RB10 / RE2 / RE3 / RE4 / RE5 > Berlin Potsdamer Platz Bahnhof

 200 / 300 / M41 / M48 / M85 / N2 > Varian-Fry-Straße/ Potsdamer Platz

The two towers designed by RPBW are part of the masterplan competition won by the firm in 1992. These two vertical skyscrapers are two of the RPBW architectural elements that stand out against the Berlin skyline, directly overlooking Potsdamer Platz. Forum Tower, also known as PwC Tower, is a 19-floor building, 78 metres high, with a sharp profile that follows the shape of the triangular plot. The glass section that projects over the plaza is supported by a brick colonnade, visible from the exterior, linked with the brick-clad building at the rear, that integrates with the rest of the masterplan. Debis-Haus, recently renamed Atrium Tower, is the tenth tallest skyscraper in the city with a height of 106 metres. Constructed in glass, steel and brick like the nearby Forum Tower, Atrium Tower is composed of five parallelepiped elements of different heights. The façade overlooking the street features windows with rounded corners set into the solid reddish structure.

© Renzo Piano Building Workshop

architects
Renzo Piano Building
Workshop

type
offices

construction
2000

72. The Feuerle Collection

Hallesches Ufer 70
10963 Berlin

Thu / 6 pm - 7 pm
Fri / 2 pm - 7 pm
Sat - Sun / 11 am - 7 pm

+49 (0) 30 25 79 23 20
dm@thefeuerlecollection.org
www.thefeuerlecollection.org

 U2 / U1 / U3 / U7
> U Mendelssohn-
Bartholdy-Park;
U Möckernbrücke

 S1 / S2 / S25 / S26 >
Anhalter Bahnhof

 M29 / N1 >
U Mendelssohn-
Bartholdy-Park

Like the air-raid shelter transformed to house the Boros Collection, The Feuerle Collection building is a converted bunker that has been restored to display the private Fuerle collection of antique Asian artefacts and contemporary avant-garde art. The former Second World War bunker covers an area of 6,480 square metres and the restoration intervention was limited to a minimum; the previous disturbing atmosphere has been transformed into a space of contemplation, thanks to the white and grey painted walls and large mirrors that reflect the interior elements. In 2017, three new sensory rooms were opened dedicated to ancient rituals. The first, the Silence Room, to which access is permitted only with phones switched off, is focussed on immersion in a minimalist music work by John Cage. The second, the Lake Room, will contain a lake that will heat the building using a geothermal heat pump, while the third, the Incense Room, reveals the traditional imperial ritual of incense burning.

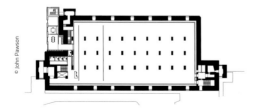

© John Pawson

architect
John Pawson

type
art gallery

construction
2017

73. Park am Gleisdreieck

Möckernstraße 26
10963 Berlin

open to the public

 U7 > Yorckstraße

 S1 / S2 / S25 / S26 >
Yorckstraße

 M19 / N7 >
Yorckstraße

This park was the winner of the Deutschen Landschaftsarchitektur-Preis 2015 (German Architecture and Landscaping Prize 2015) for the quality of its design and construction, as well as the careful choice of urban fixtures. It is located on the Gleisdreieck railway hub, abandoned ever since the Second World War. Some of the important elements are the natural wild flower meadows and the historic traces of the previous infrastructures. Towards the south are cast iron columns that support 15 bridges (a heritage monument since 1993) which mark the boundary of the area with the Yorckstraße under-passage. Here, wide Corten staircases and a long ramp give access to the park. The other entrance is the Möckerpromenade, a parkway that runs in front of the German Museum of Technology and the Bohnsdorfer Park Museum. Very long wooden benches and rounded edge paving emphasise the entrance to the vast central lawn, an essential element in every northern European park. The sober geometrical division of this immense zone is created with the use of different materials and colours: sand, gravel, stone chips, concrete, and wood.

© Atelier Loidl

architects
Atelier Loidl

type
public park

construction
2011

74. Freie Univërsitat Berlin (library)

Habelschwerdter Allee 45
14195 Berlin

Mon - Fri / 9 am - 6 pm
Sat - Sun / closed

info@philbib.fu-berlin.de
www.fu-berlin.de

 U3 > Freie Universität

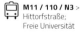 **M11 / 110 / N3** >
Hittorfstraße;
Freie Universität

The library for the Faculty of Philology is perhaps the least known of Foster + Partners' architectural works in Berlin. It is located inside the university courtyard surrounded by the Corten clad building by Jean Prouvé, based on the 'Modulor' proportional system. The Library which has been named "The Brain", is composed of various floors with serpentine balcony profiles that recede and project in an irregular manner. Over 700,000 volumes are preserved in the 11 Free University institutes. The four balconied floors house 600 reading and study desks, and are arranged to resemble a cranium or skull when seen in cross section. They are contained inside a large dome structure with a radial geometry uniting six of the university courtyards, and covered by a translucent membrane. The structure is composed of a double shell: the external layer is clad in glimmering silver aluminium panels and insulating glass that provides natural ventilation. The interior is lined with a white glass fibre fabric that allows the passage of diffused natural light for improved reading comfort.

© Foster + Partners

| **architects** | **type** | **construction** |
| Foster + Partners | library | 2005 |

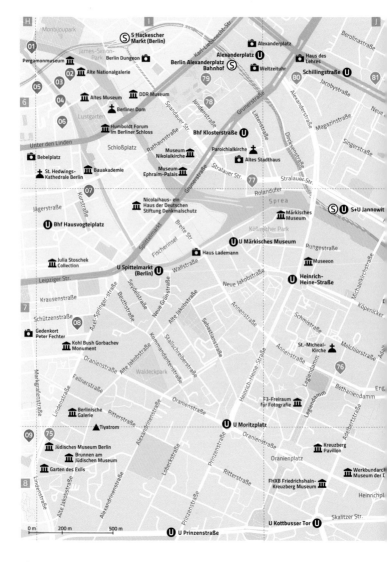

S Hackescher Markt (Berlin)

Alexanderplatz

Pergamonmuseum

Berlin Dungeon

Alte Nationalgalerie

Alexanderplatz
Berlin Alexanderplatz
Bahnhof S

Weltzeituhr

Haus des Lehres

Schillingstraße

Berolinastraße

Jacobystraße

Neue

01
02
03
05
04
06

Altes Museum

DDR Museum

Berliner Dom

Humboldt Forum
Im Berliner Schloss

79

78

80

81

Montbijoupark

James-Simon-Park

Lustgarten

Schloßplatz

Karl-Liebknecht-Str.

Spandauer Str.

Lindenstraße

Grunerstraße

Alexanderstraße

Littenstraße

Magazinstraße

Singerstraße

Bhf Klosterstraße

Bebelplatz

St. Hedwigs-
Kathedrale Berlin

Bauakademie

Museum Nikolaikirche

Museum Ephraim-Palais

Paroichialkirche

Altes Stadthaus

Dircksenstraße

Unter den Linden

Rathausstraße

Stralauer Str.

Stralauer Str.

77

Rolandufer

S p r e a

S U S+U Jannowit

07

Nicolaihaus- ein
Haus der Deutschen
Stiftung Denkmalschutz

Märkisches Museum

Jägerstraße

Kurstraße

Bhf Hausvogteiplatz

Köllnischer Park

U Märkisches Museum

Rungestraße

Museeon

Julia Stoschek
Collection

U Spittelmarkt
(Berlin)

Haus Lademann

Leipziger Str.

Wallstraße

Neue Jakobstraße

Heinrich-
Heine-Straße

Michaelkirchstraße

Köpenicker

Krausenstraße

Schützenstraße

08

Gedenkort
Peter Fechter

Kohl Bush Gorbachev
Monument

Oranienstraße

Axel-Springer-Straße

Beuthstraße

Seydelstraße

Neue Grünstraße

Alte Jakobstraße

Kommandantenstraße

Annenstraße

Stallschreiberstraße

Sebastianstraße

Schmistraße

Annenstraße

St.-Micheal-
Kirche

Legiendamm

76

Melchiorstraße

Adalb

Waldeckpark

Feilnerstraße

Lindenstraße

Markgrafenstraße

Berlinische
Galerie

Tiyatrom

Ritterstraße

Alexandrinenstraße

Oranienstraße

Heinrich-Heine-Straße

F3-Freiraum
für Fotografie

Legiendamm

Bethaniendamm

Eng.

09
75

Jüdisches Museum Berlin

Brunnen am
Jüdischen Museum

Garten des Exils

Lindenstraße

Alte Jakobstraße

Lobeckstraße

Alexandrinenstraße

Prinzenstraße

U Moritzplatz

Oranienstraße

Oranienplatz

Ritterstraße

FHXB Friedrichshain-
Kreuzberg Museum

Kreuzberg
Pavillon

Werkbundarch
Museum der D

Adelberstraße

Heinrichpl.

0 m   200 m   500 m

U Prinzenstraße

U Kottbusser Tor U

Skalitzer Str.

H
I
J

5

6

7

8

Friedrichshain – Kreuzberg

75. Jüdisches Museum
76. Taut-Haus (Engeldamm 70)
77. Embassy of the Kingdom of the Netherlands
78. Alea 101
79. Berlin TV Tower
80. bcc Berlin Congress Center
81. Kino International
82. Ludwig-Hoffmann-Grundschule
83. Central Library Friedrichshain-Kreuzberg
84. Bonjour Tristesse
85. Hufeisensiedlung – Großsiedlung Britz
86. HTW – Hochschule für Technik und Wirtschaft Berlin

75. Jüdisches Museum

Lindenstraße 9-14
10969 Berlin

Mon - Sun / 10 am - 8 pm

+49 (0) 30 25 99 33 00

www.jmberlin.de

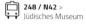
U1 / U3 / U6 >
Hallesches Tor

248 / N42 >
Jüdisches Museum

The Jewish Museum is a building charged with symbolic meaning; in an unprecedented way, it embodies the history of the Jewish people, the effects of the Holocaust, and the sense of spiritual disorientation connected with the hardships experienced through history. The building represents a deconstructed Star of David, a zinc-clad, zig-zag structure composed of fragmented horizontal planes that intersect and collide, interrupted by shards of light from the narrow slot windows that run between the roof and the façades. The concept of the museum circuit has made it famous throughout the world because of its ability to provoke intense, heart-wrenching, and uncomfortable feelings in visitors as they follow the two axial routes. The first is the route of Exile and the other, the path of Continuity: two corridors with different slopes and heights that lead to the Holocaust Tower and the Garden of Exile. The tower is a tall dark structure lit only by a small slot opening, cold in winter and suffocating in summer. The second is a square composed of 49 concrete pillars to symbolise the birth of the State of Israel, whose tops are planted with wild olive trees as a symbol of peace and the hope of a return to the homeland.

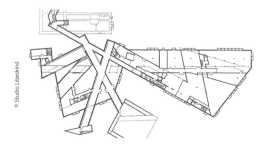

© Studio Libeskind

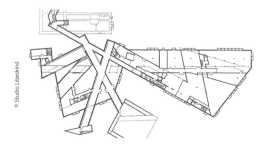

architect
Studio Libeskind

type
museum

construction
2001

76. Taut-Haus (Engeldamm 70)

Michaelkirchplatz 1
10179 Berlin

external viewing only

+49 (0) 30 80 40 90 440

www.tauthaus-am-
engelbecken.de

 U8 > U Heinrich-Heine-
Straße

 147 > Heinrich-Heine-
Platz

The headquarters of the German Transport Association, or Taut-Haus, is an office building based on the 1927 design by Bruno Taut, modified in 1929 by his brother Max. The former trade union building occupies the corner of the city block between Engeldamm Straße and Michaelkirchplatz, and is composed of a reinforced concrete structural frame with three spans per side, united by a rounded corner that softens the profile. The windows on the flat façade are positioned flush with the interior, while the top floor ribbon windows are slightly recessed, as are the large ground floor windows, in sharp contrast with the horizontal openings of the upper floors. The columns and parapets were originally clad with dark coloured stone, later replaced with shelly limestone during the reconstruction between 1949 and 1951 following war bombing. The atrium features a rounded triangular stairwell in black stone.

architect
Max Taut, Bruno Taut

type
offices, residential and offices

construction
1927-1932 (offices)
2014 (residential and offices)

77. Embassy of the Kingdom of the Netherlands

Klosterstraße 50
10179 Berlin

Mon - Fri / 9 am - 5 pm

+49 (0) 30 20 95 60
bln@minbuza.nl
www.niederlandeweltweit.nl/
laender/deutschland

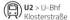 **U2** > U-Bhf
Klosterstraße

Externally, the Netherlands embassy designed by OMA is apparently a compact cube structure, but when examined more closely, it reveals a changing geometry of solids and voids with staggered profiles. The project respects the strict urban planning regulations for closing the city block curtain wall, but is interrupted by an L-shaped light well structure that surrounds two sides of the cube overlooking the Spree River. The main building, housing the office spaces and official reception rooms, features a staircase that winds around all eight floors of the building: an outstanding element that fully deserves its title of "architectural promenade" for its views over the river, the Television Tower, and the neighbourhood. The second building, less visible at first glimpse, is a parallelepiped that runs along the interior of the urban block. It forms a thick "wall" that houses the residential areas and is connected to the cube building by enclosed walkways on upper floors. The façades are clad in fine metal or mesh sheets that provide glimpses of the internal spaces. The stairways are not concealed but are a focal element of the façades, attracting attention during the day and at night for their transparency and range of colours in different zones of the building.

architect	type	construction
OMA	institutional building	2003

78. Alea 101

Rathausstraße
10178 Berlin

partially open to the public

 U2 / U5 / U8 >
Alexanderplatz

 **RB14 / RE1 / RE2 /
RE7 / S3 / S5 / S7 / S9**
> Berlin Alexanderplatz
Bahnhof

 **200 / 300 / N2 / N8
/ N40 / N42 / N65** >
Berliner Rathaus

 M4 / M5 / M6 >
S+U Alexanderplatz
Bhf/Gontardstraße

This residential and commercial building of 22,460 square metre is constructed at the foot of the Television Tower (Fernsehturm) at the centre of Berlin. The structure was developed in width rather than height to avoid conflict with the future tower buildings planned for the Alexanderplatz district. The building is composed of three urban-style, off-set, parallelepiped blocks. Each block is built with a different material with links to the nearby cityscape. On the ground floor the store windows with their slightly rounded corners act both as a screen and as connection with the plaza; the first and the second floor are clad in dark reflective material that mirrors the surrounding buildings. The uppermost box presents a structural grid of white, glass-fibre reinforced concrete that echoes the façades of the neighbouring Alexanderhaus and Berolinahaus. The third and fourth floors house offices and apartments with an internal curved façade surrounding a green planted terrace.

© Sauerbruch Hutton

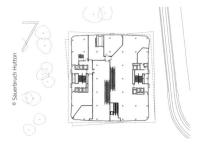

architect
Sauerbruch Hutton

type
multi-purpose building

construction
2014

79. Berlin TV Tower

Panoramastraße 1A
10178 Berlin

March - October
Mon - Sun / 9 am - 12 am
November - February
Mon - Sun / 10 am - 12 am

www.tv-turm.de

 **DPN / RB14 / RE1
/ RE2 / RE7 / S3
/ S5 / S7 / S9 >**
Berlin Alexanderplatz
Bahnhof

 RE1 / RE7 > Berlin
Alexanderplatz
Bahnhof

 M4 / M5 / M6 >
S+U Alexanderplatz
Bhf/Gontardstraße

Together with the Brandenburg Gate and the Reichstag, the television tower in the Alexanderplatz is one of the most prominent points on the Berlin skyline. 368 metres high, it is one of the tallest constructions in Germany and the fourth highest in Europe. It was built in the 1960s to showcase the technological power and efficacy of the GDR socialist system, and became the tangible symbol of the new German Democratic Republic. The famous profile is composed of a supporting column that conceals an elevator weighing 26,000 tons and that travels up 248.78 metres. It is crowned with a steel sphere composed of 120 pre-assembled segments; the sphere contains a restaurant and panoramic viewing terrace. The tower is topped with the striking red and white antenna that was mounted the year after the assembly of the sphere.

architect
Hermann Henselmann

type
television aerial, viewpoint,
restaurant

construction
1965-1969

80. bcc Berlin Congress Center

Alexanderstraße 11
10178 Berlin

open to the public

+49 (0) 30 23 80 60
info@bcc-berlin.de
www.bcc-berlin.de

 U2 / U5 / U8 >
U Alexanderplatz

 300 > S+U
Alexanderplatz/
Grunerstraße

The Berlin Congress Center is a magnificent example of Modernist architecture that has been able to withstand the test of time because of its classical composition and clever functional space layout. The building is composed of two intersecting structures, creating a dialogue of proportions, solids, voids, and transparent façades. The large central body is contained within a square two-storey structure with a steel and glass façade that reveals the graceful internal spiral staircases. The cylindrical structure is roofed with a steel dome. It has an audience capacity of over 1,000 and is clad with elegant concave panelling for a refined decor as well as providing excellent acoustics and a decorative collar on the upper wall border. The pavilion contains over 3,000 square metres of office and exhibition spaces spread through 30 rooms. After temporary closure during the 1990s, the historic building was re-opened in 2003 following extensive renovation work.

architect
Hermann Henselmann,
Kerk-Oliver Dahm

type
congress centre

construction
1964

81. Kino International

Karl-Marx-Allee 33
10178 Berlin

open to the public

+49 (0) 30 24 75 60 11
event@kino-international.com
www.kino-international.com

 U5 > Schillingstraße

 N5 > Schillingstraße

The Kino International, considered the most elegant cinema in the city, is a historical heritage building. Built between 1961 and 1964, this refined Modernist theatre stood against the backdrop of the Berolina Hotel, a tall blue parallelepiped demolished in 1995, and later reconstructed in contemporary style. Today it houses the Mitte Municipality. The theatre is composed of a parallelepiped structure that extends out nine metres over the main entrance. It features two materials: stone for the plinth base, and exposed concrete for the slightly undulating cantilevered element, whose side façades are decorated with relief sculptures by Waldemar Grzimek, Hubert Schievelbein and Karl-Heinz Schamal. The main façade is an entire wall of full height windows that flood the main foyer with natural light. It leads to the projection theatre that can seat 600 spectators. The theatre is clad in wood, with intense blue curtains and an undulated light system that covers the whole theatre ceiling.

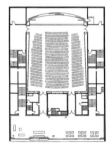

architect	type	construction
Josef Kaiser	cinema	1961-1963

82. Ludwig-Hoffmann-Grundschule

Lasdehner Straße 21
10243 Berlin

external viewing only

+49 (0) 30 29 34 74 211

www.ludwig-hoffmann-
grundschule.de

 U5 > U Frankfurter Tor

 240 / 347 / N40 >
Wedekindstraße

 21 / M10 >
U Frankfurter Tor

This elementary school was built combining the latest architectural techniques with the new educational models requested by the clients. The classrooms are connected with the public areas, corridors and protected playgrounds, and the school was attached to the existing building, the home of Ludwig Hoffmann. The internal structure was deliberately designed to expand the corridor space to form communicating areas and a connection with the rest of the structure. This design eliminates the standard escape route concept by developing a much wider corridor to form a small atrium connecting all the floors, based on the central courtyard principle. The Ludwig Hoffmann School has adopted the same clinker construction style of the main building, the Hoffman home, developing it even further to visually integrate it with the rest of the school complex. The play of shade created by the recessed clinker pattern recalls the shadows of the surrounding trees, to give a dynamic and playful effect.

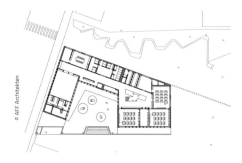

© AFF Architekten

architect
AFF Architekten

type
school

construction
2013

83. Central Library Friedrichshain-Kreuzberg

Frankfurter Allee 14A
10247 Berlin

Mon - Thu / 10 am - 7 pm
Fri / 10 am - 5 pm
Sat / 11 am - 4 pm

+49 (0) 30 90 29 85 750

 U5 > U Frankfurter Tor

 21 / M10 >
U Frankfurter Tor

The redevelopment project to transform a school into a Municipal Library was achieved by modifying the relationship of the pre-existing building with its urban context. The façades were clad with vertical wooden slats set at different angles on each floor. The colour of the wood has a dual purpose: it gives the structure a monolithic effect, while blending with the surrounding trees. The previous ribbon windows were replaced with full height square windows with dark aluminium frames. The substructure of the new façade consists of a cedar wood framework fitted to the building by means of steel brackets. This timber framework is filled with thermal insulation material in mineral wool and concealed by black façade strips so that it merges completely into the background.

architect
Peter W. Schmidt Architekten

type
library

construction
2010

84. Bonjour Tristesse

Schlesische Straße 7
10997 Berlin

external viewing only

 U1 / U3 >
Schlesisches Tor

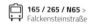 **165 / 265 / N65 >**
Falckensteinstraße

Wohnhaus Schlesisches Tor, is better known as "Bonjour Tristesse" because of the words in graffiti on the front façade, a clear reference to the existentialist novel by Françoise Sagan (1954). This was the first building constructed outside Portugal by Álvaro Siza. It was the winning project in a competition held by IBA to redevelop a large urban block in Kreuzberg that had been in a state of abandon for years, and was surrounded by the Wall on three sides. The building completes the curtain wall of the city block, maintaining alignment with the adjacent buildings. The severe lines of the rectangular grid windows are in strong contrast with the curved façades that attract the attention of passers-by. There is no ornamentation other than the eye-shaped opening on the curved gable that looks towards East Berlin, and the angular projection on the ground floor supported by a slightly crooked slender pillar. Bonjour Tristesse was designed as a seven floor apartment building, with retail stores on the ground floor. The upper floors contain 46 small social housing apartments, structured to respect the personal life style of the Turkish community.

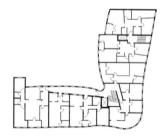

architect
Álvaro Siza Vieira,
Peter Brinkert

type
residential

construction
1980-1987

85. Hufeisensiedlung – Großsiedlung Britz

Lowise-Reuter-Ring 1
12359 Berlin

external viewing only

+49 (0) 30 89 78 60

 U7 > Parchimer Allee

 M46 / 171 / N7 >
Parchimer Allee;
Onkel-Herse-Straße

The Hufeisensiedlung (literally "Horseshoe Estate") and Britz housing estates are the maximum representation of Taut's social democratic ambition to provide a home for all, designed with the most modern housing solutions of the period, surrounded by green spaces and far from the frozen style of the typical Berlin residential buildings. Among the various estates, Haufeisensiedlung is without a doubt one of the most famous. The composition of the complex follows the topography of the area, its curved profile wrapped around a natural hollow and pond in the centre of the site. The semicircular curtain wall is 350 metres long with three storeys above ground. To the west, behind the Hufeisen, is the Britz estate, adapted to the sloping site, with terraced, one or two floor, single family homes arranged around a diamond shaped plaza. Here, Taut redeveloped the urban planning ideas of Unwin's and Howard's Garden cities. An interesting aspect is the so-called "red front" houses, characteristic for their deep red façades interrupted by the projecting stairwells painted pink.

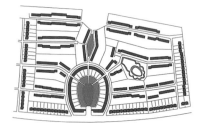

architect	**type**	**construction**
Bruno Taut, Martin Wagner	residential	1925-1927

86. HTW – Hochschule für Technik und Wirtschaft Berlin

Wilhelminenhofstraße 75A
12459 Berlin

Mon - Fri / 6.30 pm - 10 pm
Sat / 6.30 am - 6 pm

+49 (0) 30 50 190

www.htw-berlin.de

The renovation project for the public spaces at the University of Applied Sciences for Engineering and Economics, was designed to separate the public areas from those destined for the classrooms and laboratories. The regenerated spaces open to the public were created in the gaps and connecting areas between the different university pavilions, and were united to create a single coherent route down to the river bank. The paths are indicated by a minimal paving design using grey Serena stone and yellow brick. Leisure areas have been created in the former parking zone, now replaced by large green lawns and long concrete tables and benches for student use at mealtimes.

 N67 > Rathenaustraße/
HTW

 27 / 37 / 60 / 61 / 67
> Rathenaustraße/
HTW

architect
Lützow 7 (landscape
architects), Nalbach
und Nalbach Architekten

type
park (university campus)

construction
2009

Museums

AlliiertenMuseum
20th Century History Museum
-
Clayallee 135, 14195 Berlin

www.alliiertenmuseum.de
info@alliiertenmuseum.de
+49 (0) 30 81 819 90

Bauhaus-Archiv Wegen
Bauhaus Museum
-
Schillerstraße 9, D-10625 Berlin

www.bauhaus.de
bauhaus@bauhaus.de
+49 (0) 30 25 400 20

Berlinische Galerie
Museum of contemporary art
-
Alte Jakobstraße 124-128, 10969 Berlin

www.berlinischegalerie.de
bg@berlinischegalerie.de
+49 (0) 30 78 902 600

Brücke-Museum
Die Brücke Artist Group Museum
-
Bussardsteig 9- 14195 Berlin

www.bruecke-museum.de
info@bruecke-museum.de
+49 (0) 30 83 900 860

Deutsches Historisches Museum
German history museum
-
Unter den Linden 2, 10117 Berlin

www.dhm.de
fuehrung@dhm.de
+49 (0) 30 20 304 0

Deutsches Technikmuseum
Science and Technology Museum
-
Trebbiner Straße 9, 10963 Berlin

www.technikmuseum.berlin
info@technikmuseum.berlin
+49 (0) 30 90 254 0

Deutsche Kinemathek –
Museum für Film und Fernsehen
Film Archives, Cinema and
Television Museum
-
Potsdamer Straße 2, D-10785 Berlin

www.deutsche-kinemathek.de
info@deutsche-kinemathek.de
+49 (0) 30 30 090 30

Gedenkstätte Berliner Mauer
Berlin Wall Memorial
-
Bernauer Straße 119, 13355 Berlin

www.berliner-mauer-gedenkstaette.de
info@stiftung-berliner-mauer.de
+49 (0) 30 21 308 5166

Jüdisches Museum
Jewish museum
-
Lindenstraße 9-14, 10969 Berlin

www.berlin.de
info@berlin.de
+49 (0) 30 25 993 300

Märkisches Museum
Berlin City Museum
-
Poststraße 13-14, 10178 Berlin

www.stadtmuseum.de
info@stadtmuseum.de
+49 (0) 30 24 002 162

Museum in der Kulturbrauerei
Museum of contemporary history
-
Knaackstraße 97, 10435 Berlin

www.hdg.de/museum-in-der-kulturbrauerei
post@hdg.de
+49 (02 28) 91 650

Museum für Naturkunde
Natural history museum
-
Invalidenstraße 43, 10115 Berlin

www.museumfuernaturkunde.berlin
info@mfn.berlin
+49 (0) 30 889140-8591

C/O Berlin
Photography and Visual Media Museum
-
Hardenbergstraße 22-24, 10623 Berlin

www.co-berlin.org
info@co-berlin.org
+49 (0) 30 28 444 1662

Mauermuseum Haus am Checkpoint Charlie
Museum of the Berlin Wall years at the
famous checkpoint Charlie border between
East and West Berlin
-
Friedrichstraße 43-45, 10969 Berlin

www.mauermuseum.de
info@mauermuseum.de
+49 (0) 30 253 72 50

Futurium
Centre for projecting the future
-
Alexanderufer 2, 10117 Berlin

www.futurium.de
office@futurium.de
+49 (0) 30 40 818 970

Sammlung Boros
Boros Contemporary Art Collection
-
Bunker, Reinhardtstraße 20, 10117 Berlin

www.sammlung-boros.de
info@sammlung-boros.de
+49 (0) 30 27 594 065

East Side Gallery
Original remaining Berlin Wall route
-
Mühlenstraße 3-100, 10243 Berlin

www.eastsidegallery-berlin.com
info@eastsidegallery-berlin.com

The Feuerle Collection
Contemporary Art and Antiques Museum
-
Hallesches Ufer 70, 10963 Berlin

www.thefeuerlecollection.org
info@thefeuerlecollection.org
+49 (0) 30 25 79 23 20

Topographie des Terrors
Topography of Terror (Nazi) Museum
-
Niederkirchnerstraße 8, 10963 Berlin

www.topographie.de
info@topographie.de
+49 (0) 30 25 45 09-70

Tränenpalast
Berlin City History Museum (1962 to 1990)
-
Tränenpalast Reichstagufer 17, 10117 Berlin

www.hdg.de/traenenpalast
besucherdienst-berlin@hdg.de
+49 (0) 30 46 77 77 9-11

Berghain Boros
Temporary museum of contemporary art
(Boros collection)
-
Am Wriezener Bahnhof, 10243 Berlin

www.berghain.berlin
support@berghain.de
+49 (0) 30 29 35 18 10

Museumsinsel
Pergamonmuseum Archaeological Museum
Neues Museum Archaeological Museum
Alte Nationalgalerie Museum of 19th
Century Art
Altes Museum Museum of ancient art
Bode-Museum Museum of antique art
and sculpture, coins and medals
-
Bodestraße 1-3, 10178 Berlin;
Am Kupfergraben, 10117 Berlin

www.smb.museum
kommunikation@smb.spk-berlin.de
+49 (0) 30 26 642 4242

Gemäldegalerie
Art Gallery of 13th to 18th Century Art
-
Matthäikirchplatz, 10785 Berlin

www.smb.museum
kommunikation@smb.spk-berlin.de
+49 (0) 30 26 642 4242

Hamburger Bahnhof
Museum of contemporary art
-
Invalidenstraße 50-51, 10557 Berlin

www.smb.museum
kommunikation@smb.spk-berlin.de
+49 (0) 30 26 642 4242

Museum Europäischer Kulturen
Ethnological Museum
-
Arnimallee 25, 14195 Berlin

www.smb.museum
kommunikation@smb.spk-berlin.de
+49 (0) 30 26 642 4242

Museum für Fotografie
Photography Museum
-
Jebensstraße 2, 10623 Berlin

www.smb.museum
kommunikation@smb.spk-berlin.de
+49 (0) 30 26 642 4242

Neue Nationalgalerie
Museum of contemporary art
-
Potsdamer Straße 50, 10785 Berlin

www.smb.museum
kommunikation@smb.spk-berlin.de
+49 (0) 30 26 642 4242

Theatres

Berliner Ensemble
-
Bertolt-Brecht-Platz 1, 10117 Berlin

www.berliner-ensemble.de
presseassistenz@berliner-ensemble.de
+49 (0) 30 284 081 55

Schaubuehne
-
Kurfürstendamm 153, 10709 Berlin

www.schaubuehne.de
ticket@schaubuehne.de
+49 (0) 30 890 020

Admiralspalast
-
Friedrichstraße 101, 10117 Berlin

www.admiralspalast.theater
kontakt@mehr.de
+49 (0) 30 225 070 00

Chamaeleon
-
Rosenthaler Straße 40/41, in den
Hackeschen Höfen, 10178 Berlin

www.chamaeleonberlin.com
info@chamaeleonberlin.com
+49 (0) 30 400 05 90

Komische Oper
-
Behrenstraße 55-57, 10117 Berlin

www.komische-oper-berlin.de

+49 (0) 30 479 974 00

Neuköllner Oper
-
Karl-Marx-Straße 131-133, 12043 Berlin

www.neukoellneroper.de
tickets@neukoellneroper.de
+49 (0) 30 688 907 77

Theaterhaus Mitte
-
Haus C, Wallstraße 32, 10179 Berlin

www.theaterhaus-berlin.com
vertragsbuero@thbm.de
+49 (0) 30 280 943 93

Dock 11
••
Kastanienallee 79, 10435 Berlin

www.dock11-berlin.de
ticket@dock11-berlin.de
+49 (0) 30 351 203 12

Deutsches Theater Berlin
-
Schumannstraße 13 A10117 Berlin

www.deutschestheater.de
service@deutschestheater.de
+49 (0) 30 284 410

Restaurants

Taverna To Koutouki (Greek)
••
Kottbusser Damm 9, 10967 Berlin

www.koutoukionlinebestellen.com
koutoukionlinebestellen@yahoo.com
+49 (0) 30 692 521 7

••• expensive
•• mid-range
• inexpensive

**Berkis Griechische Restaurants Berlin
(Greek)**
•
Winterfeldtstrasse 45, 10781 Berlin

www.berkis.de
winterfeldtplatz@berkis.de
+49 (0) 30 779 00 402

Wirthaus Heuberger (Bavarian)
∙∙
Gotenstraße 1, 10829 Berlin

www.wirtshaus-heuberger.de
reservierung@wirtshaus-heuberger.de
+49 (0) 30 78 95 73 37

Berliner Republik - Brokers Bierbörse (currywurst)
∙
Schiffbauerdamm 8, 10117 Berlin

www.die-berliner-republik.de
info@die-berliner-republik.de
+49 (0) 30308 722 93

Freischwimmer
∙∙
Vor dem Schlesischen Tor 2a, 10997 Berlin

www.freischwimmer-berlin.com
ahoi@freischwimmer-berlin.com
+49 (0) 30 610 743 09

Clärchens Ballhaus
∙∙
Auguststraße 24, 10117 Berlin

www.ballhaus.de
reservierungen@ballhaus.de
+49 (0) 30 868 02 132

5-cinco by Paco Pérez (Michelin star)
∙∙∙
Drakestraße 1, 10787 Berlin

www.5-cinco.com
5@das-stue.com
+49 (0) 30 311 722-0

Pauly Saal (Michelin star)
∙∙∙
Auguststraße 11, 10115 Berlin

www.paulysaal.com
office@paulysaal.com
+49 (0) 30 3300 6070

Lorenz Adlon (Michelin star)
∙∙∙
Unter den Linden 77, 10117 Berlin

www.lorenzadlon-esszimmer.de
lorenz.adlon@kempinski.com
+49 (0) 30 2261 1960

Hugos (Michelin star)
∙∙∙
Budapester Straße 2, 10787 Berlin

www.hugos-restaurant.de
mail@hugos-restaurant.de
+49 (0) 30 260 212 63

Golvet (Michelin star)
∙∙∙
Potsdamer Straße 58, 10785 Berlin

www.golvet.de
info@golvet.de
+49 (0) 30 890 642 22

Facil (Michelin star)
∙∙∙
Potsdamer Straße 3, 10785 Berlin

www.facil.de
welcome@facil.de
+49 (0) 30 590 051 234

einsunternull (Michelin star)
∙∙∙
Hannoversche Straße 1, 10115 Berlin

www.restaurant-einsunternull.de
kontakt@einsunternull.com
+49 (0) 30 27 57 78 10

Spätzle und Knödel (German)
∙∙
Wühlischstraße 20, 10247 Berlin

www.spaetzleknoedel.de
info@spaetzleknoedel.de
+49 (0) 30 27 57 11 51

Chutnify Pberg (Indian)
∙∙
Sredzkistraße 43, 10435 Berlin

www.chutnify.com
hello@chutnify.com
+49 (0) 351 937 496 262

Hotels

Hotel Berlin
••
Lützowplatz 17, 10785 Berlin

www.hotel-berlin.de
info@hotel-berlin.de
+49 (0) 30 260 50

••• expensive
•• mid-range
• inexpensive

Nhow Berlin
••
Stralauer Allee 3, 10245 Berlin

www.nhow-hotels.com/en/nhow-berlin/
berlin@nhow-hotels.com
+49 (0) 30 290 299 0

25hours Hotel
••
Budapester Straße 40, 10787 Berlin

www.25hours-hotels.com/hotels/berlin/
bikini-berlin
bikini@25hours-hotels.com
+49 (0) 30 12 02 21 0

Hotel Adlon Kempinski
•••
Unter den Linden 77, 10117 Berlin

www.kempinski.com
hotel.adlon@kempinski.com
+49 (0) 30 226 10

Quentin Berlin
••
Xantener Straße 4, 10707 Berlin

www.quentinberlin.com
berlin@quentinhotels.com
+49 (0) 30 343 52 60

Sheraton Berlin Grand Hotel Esplanade
•••
Lützowufer 15, 10785 Berlin

www.esplanade.de
info@sheratonberlinesplanade.com
+49 (0) 30 254 780

a&o Hostel Berlin Hauptbahnhof
•
Lehrter Straße 12, 10557 Berlin

www.aohostels.com

+49 (0) 30 322 920 420 0

Das Andere Haus VIII
•
Erich-Mueller-Straße 12, 10317 Berlin

www.dasanderehaus8.de
info@dasanderehaus8.de
+49 (0) 30 554 403 31

Das DDR Hostel
•
Wriezener Karree 5, 10243 Berlin

Eastern Comfort Hostelboats
••
Mühlenstraße 73, 10243 Berlin

www.eastern-comfort.com
captn@eastern-comfort.com
+49 (0) 306 676 380 6

Architectural offices

Bellmann Gesellschaft von Architekten
Hochkirchstraße 5, 10829 Berlin

www.bellmannarchitekten.de
info@bellmannarchitekten.de
+49 (0) 30 282 32 14

Atelier Loidl
Am Tempelhofer Berg 6, 10965 Berlin

www.atelier-loidl.de
office@atelier-loidl.de
+49 (0) 30 300 244 50

Barkow Leibinger
Schillerstraße 94, 10625 Berlin

www.barkowleibinger.com
info@barkowleibinger.com
+49 (0) 30 315 71 20

Brandlhuber+
Brunnenstraße 9, 10119 Berlin

www.brandlhuber.com
team@brandlhuber.com
+49 (0) 30 473 775 30

Schultes Frank Architekten
Lützowplatz 7, 10785 Berlin

www.schultesfrank.de
office@schultesfrank.de
+49 (0) 30 230 888 0

LANGHOF
Oranienburger Straße 27, 10117 Berlin

www.langhof.com
berlin@langhof.com
+49 (0) 30 884 798 0

COORDINATION
Bülowstraße 56, 10783 Berlin

www.coordination-design.com
post@coordination-berlin.com
+49 (0) 30 206 073 88 00

David Chipperfield Architects
Joachimstraße 11, 10119 Berlin

davidchipperfield.com/people/berlin
info@davidchipperfield.de
+49 (0) 30 280 170 0

Deadline
Hessische Straße 5, 0115 Berlin

www.deadline.de
post@deadline.de
+49 (0) 30 285 999 34

Diener & Diener Architekten
Rosenthaler Straße 40/41, 10178 Berlin

www.dienerdiener.ch
buero.berlin@dienerdiener.de
+49 (0) 30 285 39 810

Fugmann Janotta Partner
Belziger Straße 25, 10823 Berlin

www.fugmannjanotta.de
buero@fjp.berlin
+49 (0) 30 700 119 60

Schlaich Bergermann Partner
Brunnenstraße 110c, 13355 Berlin

www.sbp.de
berlin@sbp.de
+49 (0) 30 814 528 30

Hans Kollhoff
Fasanenstraße 70, D-10719 Berlin

www.kollhoff.de
buero@kollhoff.de
+49 (0) 30 884 18 50

Helmut Jahn
Bellevuestraße 5, 10785 Berlin

www.jahn-us.com
info@jahn-us.com
+49 (0) 30 257 518 80

DAHM Architekten + Ingenieure GmbH
Mühlenstraße 34, 10243 Berlin

www.dahm-ai.de
box@dahm-ai.de
+49 (0) 30 293 690 30

huber staudt architekten
Keithstraße 2-4, 10787 Berlin

www.huberstaudtarchitekten.de
info@huberstaudtarchitekten.de
+49 (0) 30 880 010 80

J. MAYER H. und Partner, Architekten
Zementhaus Knesebeckstraße 30,
10623 Berlin

www.jmayerh.de
contact@jmayerh.de
+49 (0) 30 644 907 700

Realarchitektur
Paul-Lincke-Ufer 41, 10999 Berlin

www.realarchitektur.eu
mail@realarchitektur.de
+49 (0) 30 612 097 00

Kuehn Malvezzi
Torstraße 84, 10119 Berlin

www.kuehnmalvezzi.com
mail@kuehnmalvezzi.com
+49 (0) 30 398 068 00

léonwohlhage
Pfalzburger Straße 74, 10719 Berlin

www.leonwohlhage.de
post@leonwohlhage.de
+49 (0) 30 327 600 0

Lützow 7
Giesebrechtstraße 10, 10629 Berlin

www.luetzow7.de
infoluetzow7.de
+49 (0) 30 330 041 0

Max Dudler
Oranienplatz 4, 10999 Berlin

www.maxdudler.de
info@maxdudler.de
+49 (0) 30 615 10 73

Peter W. Schmidt Architekten
Karl-Marx-Allee 103 a, D-10243 Berlin

www.pws.eu
berlin@pws.eu
+49 (0) 302 308 610

Richter Musikowski
Ritterstraße 2, D-10969 Berlin

www.richtermusikowski.com
info@richtermusikowski.com
+49 (0) 30 202 378 74

Sauerbruch Hutton
Lehrter Straße 57, Haus 2, D-10557 Berlin

www.sauerbruchhutton.de
office@sauerbruchhutton.de
+49 (0) 30 397 8210

TCHOBAN VOSS Architekten
Rosenthaler Straße 40-41, Hackesche Höfe,
D-10178 Berlin

www.tchobanvoss.de
berlin@tchobanvoss.de
+49 (0) 30 283 920 0

zanderrotharchitekten
Dunckerstraße 63, 10439 Berlin

www.zanderroth.de
kontakt@zanderroth.de
+49 (0) 30 405 057 60

Zvi Hecker Architect
Fehrbelliner Straße 34, D-10119 Berlin

www.zvihecker.com
berlin@zvihecker.com
+49 (0) 30 275 82 670

Index by architect

Index by project

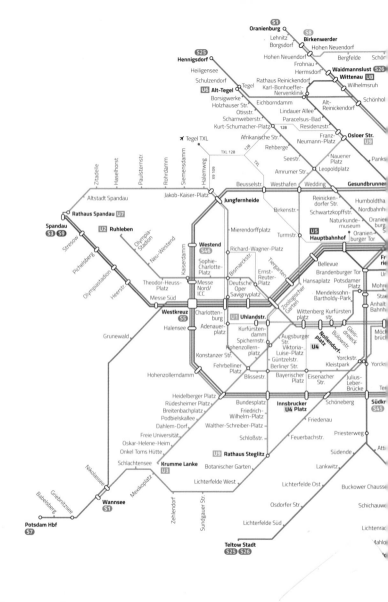